CONTENTS

DIRECTOR'S FOREWORD

SPONSOR'S FOREWORD

The world is increasingly filled with images of people, captured through security cameras or shared through Internet photo and networking sites. Such sites offer a complex mix of the random and the purposeful, but arguably they make the function of a structured photographic portrait even more significant. Promoting the very best of photographic portraiture is why the Taylor Wessing Photographic Portrait Prize matters.

Judging 6,758 photographic portraits in order to find the very best sixty for the exhibition is an exacting process. A set of judges, working together for the first time, are drawn towards an understanding of each other's preferences, interests and passions. For one judge it is an austere singular figure portrayed in a landscape which stands out; for another a chaotic urban scene sparks a response. The selection of prize-winners and exhibitors are not matters of compromise, but rather of coming to a common view of the best possible collection of outstanding images – judged anonymously – from the myriad of well-composed and technically strong submissions.

I want to thank the many gifted photographers who entered the Taylor Wessing Photographic Portrait Prize 2008. Congratulations go to this year's winners: Lottie Davies, Hendrik Kerstens, Catherine Balet and Tom Stoddart, and to the recipient of the Godfrey Argent Award, Vanessa Winship. I am grateful to the estate of Godfrey Argent for supporting a special award this year to a photographer working in black and white.

I should like to thank: my fellow judges – David A. Bailey, Michael Frawley, Julia Fullerton-Batten, Terence Pepper and Joanna Pitman – who worked with great determination and were thoughtful and passionate in their choices; Ben Okri for his insightful and thought-provoking essay; interviewer Richard McClure; Thomas Manss & Company for their exceptional design work; the white wall company for their contribution to the judging process; and the staff of the National Portrait Gallery.

Special thanks are owed to Taylor Wessing at the start of their sponsorship of the Prize. It is a strong partnership growing out of their support for the Gallery over a number of years.

SANDY NAIRNE
DIRECTOR, NATIONAL PORTRAIT GALLERY

Taylor Wessing is pleased to sponsor the Photographic Portrait Prize as it builds on our long-standing relationship with the National Portrait Gallery and, in particular, our sponsorship of The World's Most Photographed and Face of Fashion exhibitions in 2005 and 2007.

This year's competition was of a high standard, and the quality of entries was excellent. Some of the images were incredibly thought-provoking, encouraging us to consider the story behind the picture. My overall impression was of the photographers' immense talent, in both creativity and depth of vision.

The Prize is a great forum to encourage and cultivate new talent, an area that Taylor Wessing strongly supports. It works hand in hand with our goals of supporting art and culture and striving for excellence.

We are also working with the National Portrait Gallery to intro-duce parts of the exhibition to our community partners such as St Mungo's and University College London Hospitals, so that those who would not normally go to the Gallery can also benefit from this event.

On behalf of the partners at Taylor Wessing, I would like to thank the National Portrait Gallery for involving us in this project.

Finally, I hope that you enjoy the Taylor Wessing Photographic Portrait Prize 2008, a celebration of innovation within the genre of photographic portraiture today.

MICHAEL FRAWLEY
MANAGING PARTNER, TAYLOR WESSING LLP

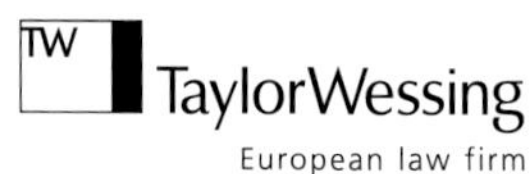

PHOTOGRAPHY AND IMMORTALITY
BEN OKRI

Photography ought to be seen as a species of magic, but we have lost our innocence. And so we see it as an aspect of reality.

There is no art by which to reproduce the lineaments of reality. Each human face will always be unique in skin, flesh and features. Any attempt at exact reproduction loses the contours, the three-dimensionality and the living quality of the individual face. What photography achieves in portraiture is not a reproduction, but a refiguration, a translation from one dimension to another.

Something strange happens in this process: the human face is alienated. It is a metamorphosis in reverse. The face is thus simplified. The curved quality of space is flattened. Light is reduced in source and effect.

Portraiture is the dialogue of light and the face, in the dimension of memory. That is why the portrait is not the person. It is an abstracted memory, enriched by time.

Three principles make portraiture unique: light, the subject, and time. Of these three, the most alchemical is time. Time is the magic mercury, the fifth element, the quintessence. It is the constantly transforming and preserving substance of portraiture.

Time acts with the shutter speed. It acts with the speed of light that travels to the subject, from the subject to the camera, and from the photograph to our eyes.

There is an internal time that is also at work from the first mental encounter with the image to its interactions in the vast realm of memory. A realm perpetually impinged on by desire, loss and life's infinitely shaded experiences.

Time weaves a spell round the image – preserves it, changes it. Portraiture keeps the subject in its time and yet projects it into ours.

Portraiture is always time travel. It is a time travel that keeps all the secrets of its time concealed behind the subject. It freights over to us only the image, mute with all the passions of life.

Silent stories stare out from those eyes. They will no longer look upon the light or dark of our day. And yet they look at us as through a transparent medium, beyond even death. What is the true nature of that almost mystic medium?

There is a hint of immortality in all portraiture. The subjects live, in another dimension, alien to us. They live, but they are motionless. Time has gone from them, yet still they persist in time. They live in an enigma.

Does their image differ from the memory we have of them? Is memory truer?

Portraiture suggests a parallel memory in the universe, in which all things persist. Photography touches us so mysteriously because we have an intuition that all things are remembered in some invisible place beyond dreams, where everything that was exists in a sort of universal, divine amber.

Many wonderful notions ought to flash past one's mind in the presence of these people upon whom time has wrought an enchantment.

Portraiture ought to remind us that we live between two enigmas, birth and death. Photography is the dream, the interval, which we take to be the real.

And yet secret tears flow behind these portraits. We too will be like them.

But we have lost our innocence. Otherwise these images ought to start in us a new philosophy of living, a new simplicity, and maybe even a new happiness.

THE PRIZES

TAYLOR WESSING PHOTOGRAPHIC PORTRAIT PRIZE

The Taylor Wessing Photographic Portrait Prize is open to photographers from around the world aged eighteen or over.

The first prize winner is Lottie Davies, who receives £12,000.

The second prize winner is Hendrik Kerstens, who receives £3,000.

The third prize winner is Catherine Balet, who receives £2,000.

The fourth prize winner is Tom Stoddart, who receives £1,000.

THE GODFREY ARGENT AWARD

The Godfrey Argent Award is given this year to the photographer of the best black-and-white portrait.

The winner is Vanessa Winship, who receives £2,500.

If you would like to join the mailing list to receive an entry form for next year's Photographic Portrait Prize, please send your full contact details to:

Photographic Portrait Prize 2009
Marketing Department
National Portrait Gallery
St Martin's Place
London WC2H 0HE

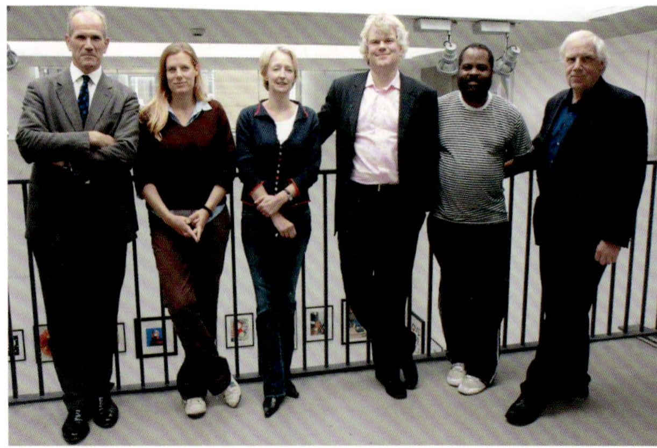

THE JUDGES, FROM LEFT TO RIGHT: SANDY NAIRNE, JULIA FULLERTON-BATTEN, JOANNA PITMAN, MICHAEL FRAWLEY, DAVID A. BAILEY, TERENCE PEPPER
PHOTOGRAPH BY CLARE FREESTONE, AUGUST 2008

THE JUDGES

CHAIR: SANDY NAIRNE,
DIRECTOR, NATIONAL PORTRAIT GALLERY
The 2008 Taylor Wessing Photographic Portrait Prize offered a fascinating overview of outstanding photographic portrait work submitted from around the globe. Every human subject seemed to be present. But there were images that stood out. And without knowing the photographer, as this is a competition judged anonymously, it was possible through close deliberation to come to a view of the best sixty to include in the exhibition and the special images to be awarded prizes. I am most grateful for the time and effort of all the photographers who submitted their work, and for the close attention paid by the judges.

DAVID A. BAILEY
CURATOR, PHOTOGRAPHER, WRITER AND LECTURER
Two things concerned me about being on the judging panel: will there be a wide range of work and will the judges be able to come to some consensus on the final selection? After viewing what seemed to be an endless list of works I could not have been more wrong. The range, the use of different photographic genres, and the attention to detail and narrative within the works were amazing. It was even more difficult when some people submitted more than one photograph of a very high quality. Though we all came from distinct photographic backgrounds and histories, we managed to agree on a final selection without it all ending in bloodshed. I believe that this had to do with the quality of the submissions which matched the prize criteria and could be seen in the context of what a twenty-first-century photographic portrait should strive to be.

MICHAEL FRAWLEY
MANAGING PARTNER, TAYLOR WESSING LLP
One of the privileges of being the sponsor of this year's Taylor Wessing Photographic Portrait Prize was being invited to join the judging panel. The thing that struck me about this year's competition was the exceptionally high quality of the entries, that made the task of selecting the shortlist of sixty photos and the eventual winners a challenge. From a personal point of view, it was interesting for me to look at the photographs (and their titles) and to imagine the story behind the picture. In some cases, the images were shocking, but all of them made an impact on me. My overall impression was of the photographers' immense talent, in both creativity and depth of vision.

JULIA FULLERTON-BATTEN
PHOTOGRAPHER
When I was invited to be a judge I thought, 'Oh no! I want to enter my own images!' But once I put the phone down I realised how privileged I would be to judge the most prestigious photographic portrait award in the UK. It was fascinating to be 'behind the scenes' and I tried hard to look at each individual image and give it a chance to get through to the next round – I know how exciting it is to receive the congratulatory letter through the post. I decided to avoid clichéd images and selected photographs that were fresh, innovative, and revealed a good eye for the subject matter. Opinions differed considerably and I was disappointed when some of my favourite images didn't make it. However, the end result is a great selection of very varied work, and I am looking forward to seeing them exhibited at the National Portrait Gallery.

TERENCE PEPPER
CURATOR OF PHOTOGRAPHS, NATIONAL PORTRAIT GALLERY
Being a judge and selector for the Taylor Wessing Photographic Portrait Prize is the highlight of the year for encountering the best and most varied selection of what photographers deem to be their finest portraits. I worked with an inspired team of fellow judges, who all brought different but informed imagination to the panel, and we quickly agreed the 300 or so front-runners from the 6,758 submitted photographs. On the second day this process was refined and refined to make the final selection a worthy mirror of contemporary photographic portraiture.

JOANNA PITMAN
PHOTOGRAPHY CRITIC FOR *THE TIMES*
It was wonderful that so many photographs had been entered, but galling that they had to be judged in two days. Had they all been brilliant pictures, the judging would of course have been much harder. There were a great number of very good photographs, and the skill was in singling out the really great from the very good. The viewing was intense, and the discussion both revealing and exhilarating and, in spite of the range of judges on the panel, I was surprised to see the extent of overlap in our choices for the final four. I found I was photo-blind for several days afterwards.

FIRST PRIZE
LOTTIE DAVIES

A photographer for the past eight years, Lottie Davies has turned her hand to most aspects of her profession, from shooting reportage features on the Kalahari Bushmen for the *Telegraph* magazine to working with chef Gary Rhodes to illustrate recipes for his cookery books. It was this strong desire to 'resist being pigeonholed' that led Davies to make her first foray into fine art photography.

That decision has borne immediate fruit with her winning entry in the Taylor Wessing Photographic Portrait Prize 2008. *Quints* is taken from *Memories and Nightmares*, a personal project aimed at creating alternative representations of her subjects as opposed to more conventional portraiture. At the beginning of 2008 Davies asked several friends to send her written accounts of either an early childhood memory or a nightmare, which then provided the basis for the ongoing series.

'We all have our own tales and myths which we use to tell our lives. In some ways, a person can be described as the total of all their stories and experiences,' she says. 'Nightmares are similar to early memories in that they can be so intense that the recollection sometimes lasts all one's life. When this happens, they become a marker, an event in a person's life, and as such, become part of them and their personal history.'

Quints depicts a nightmare described by Davies's friend, Caroline, a mother-of-two who dreamt that she gave birth to quintuplets. Drawing on classical imagery of the Madonna and Child, Davies also took inspiration from several visits to the National Gallery, replicating the darkness and colours found in Caravaggio and Titian to portray the 'calm and serenity of motherhood, as well as the feeling of imprisonment'.

Rather than asking Caroline to pose, she used a model, Alicia Clarke, to represent her friend. 'Using a model,' she explains, 'allows me more freedom to interpret the story as I like, unclouded by the representational aspects of portraiture.'

Shooting large-format with a Horseman 5x4 in a near-derelict building in east London, Davies took multiple frames of a 10-week-old baby, Marla, who is Alicia's niece. She then combined the different frames in post-production to achieve the final image. 'I still enjoy traditional portraiture but I do think there is space to play with and expand on the idea of representation of people and of things. That, to me, is the purpose of image-making.'

INTERVIEW BY RICHARD MCCLURE

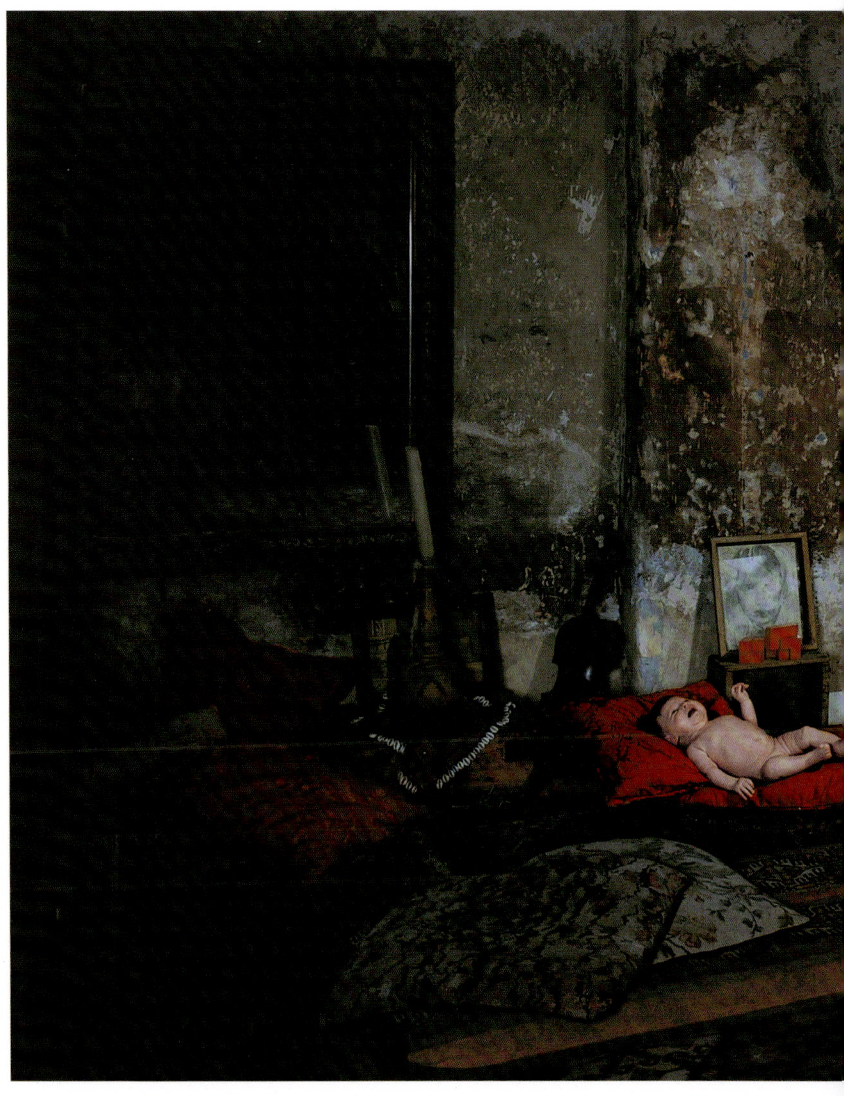

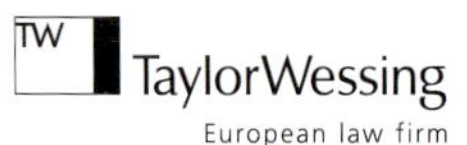

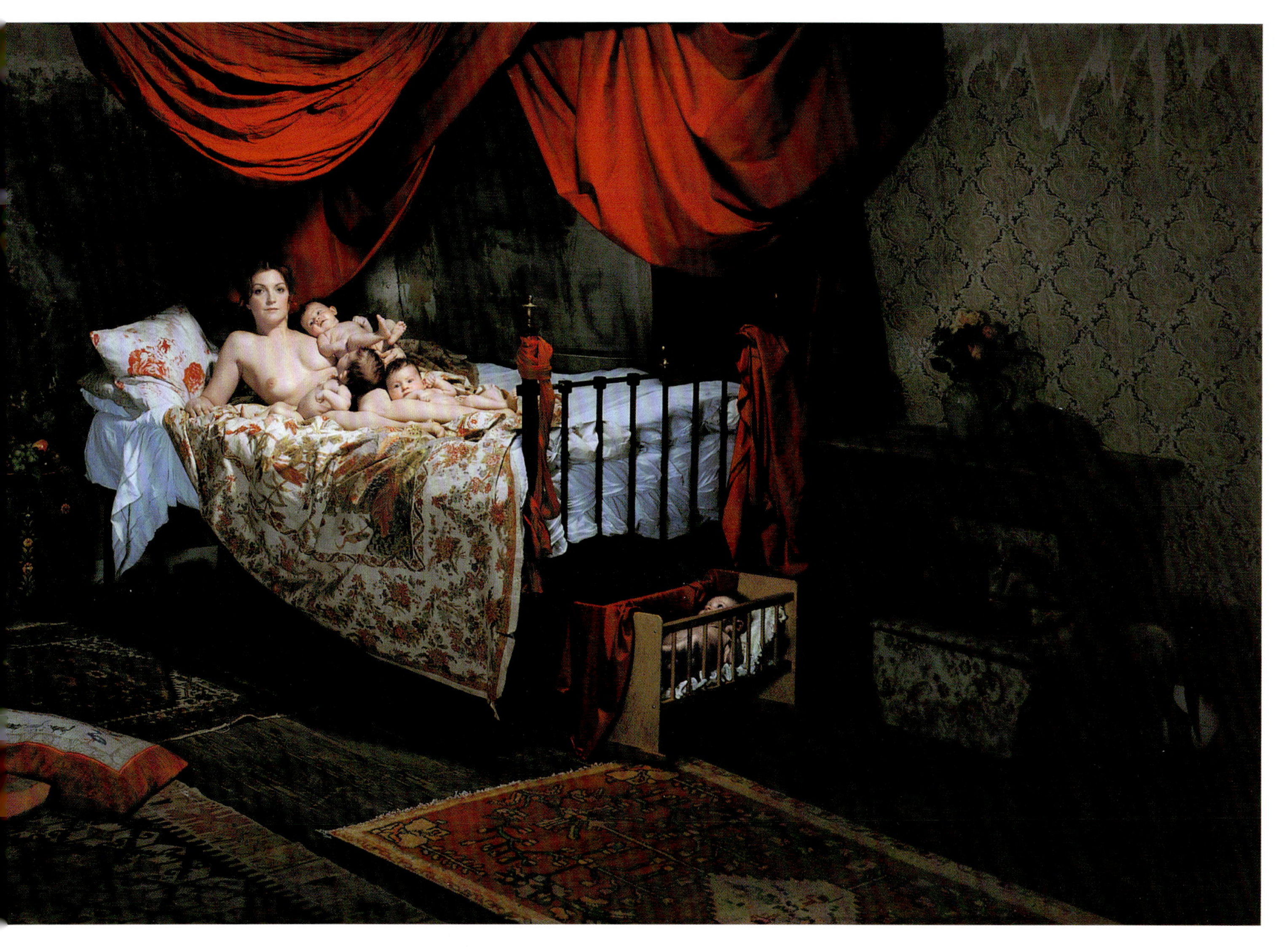

LOTTIE DAVIES
QUINTS
FROM THE SERIES
MEMORIES AND NIGHTMARES
MARCH 2008

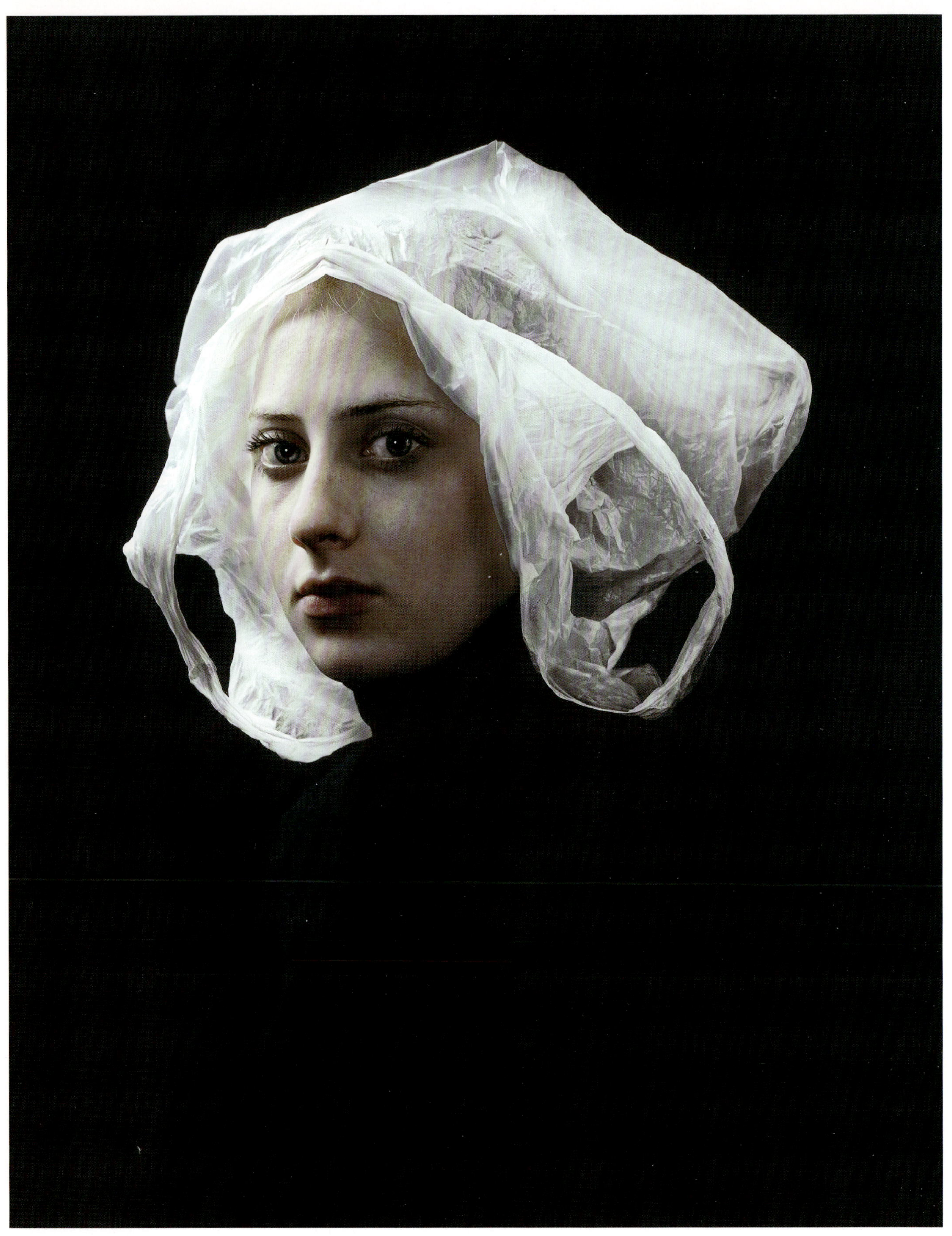

HENDRIK KERSTENS

BAG

NOVEMBER 2007

SECOND PRIZE
HENDRIK KERSTENS

Like many first-time fathers, Hendrik Kerstens was compelled to pick up a camera following the birth of his daughter Paula. What began as a paternal impulse to record her childhood has since become a photographic fixation for Kerstens, who has used Paula as both model and muse for almost all his portraiture.

In 1995 he quit his career as an Amsterdam wine dealer to pursue photography professionally. 'Dealing in wine was very nice, but I felt dissatisfied creatively,' he explains. 'I had started to photograph Paula purely for my own pleasure, with no intention of becoming an artist. I simply wanted to capture those fleeting moments that fade from the memory all too quickly. Paula is my only child so photography is a way to keep her close, a way to keep her childhood with me while she is becoming an adult woman. It's also a way to deal with my fear of losing her.'

Following positive critical reaction to his work, the 52-year-old is now represented by Amsterdam's Witzenhausen Gallery and has exhibited his photographs of Paula, now aged twenty-one, across Europe and the USA. 'I'm self-taught and my photography is really a family business as my wife works with me as an assistant,' he says. 'As Paula has become older, she has become more involved in the process. We do talk about my work but it does not influence my artistic freedom to photograph her the way I want to. She likes being photographed; she always has done.'

Taken with a Toyo-View 8x10 camera, many of the portraits consciously evoke seventeenth-century northern European painting, in particular the art of Johannes Vermeer, with bonnets and wimples replaced by modern clothing and other twenty-first-century accessories. Originally influenced by the 'classical purity' of Robert Mapplethorpe, Kerstens developed his signature style when Paula returned from horseback riding one day. 'She took off her cap and I was struck by the image of her hair held together by a hair-net. It reminded me of the portraits by the Dutch Masters and I started to take more photographs which refer to the paintings of that era.'

His latest work addresses the question 'of how Paula will be living in her environment by the time she reaches my age'. As part of that theme, *Bag* was taken following a trip to New York where the eco-conscious Kerstens was appalled by the excessive use of plastic shopping bags, one of which features in the picture as slyly humorous headgear.

'Northern European painting relies on craftsmanship and the perfect rendition of the subject, and the use of light is instrumental in this,' says Kerstens. 'A lot of people think I get the painterly effect by manipulating the image somehow. I don't. The lighting is all done in the studio. Taking someone today and portraying her in the style of these artists is a way for me to shake up the concept of time.'

INTERVIEW BY RICHARD MCCLURE

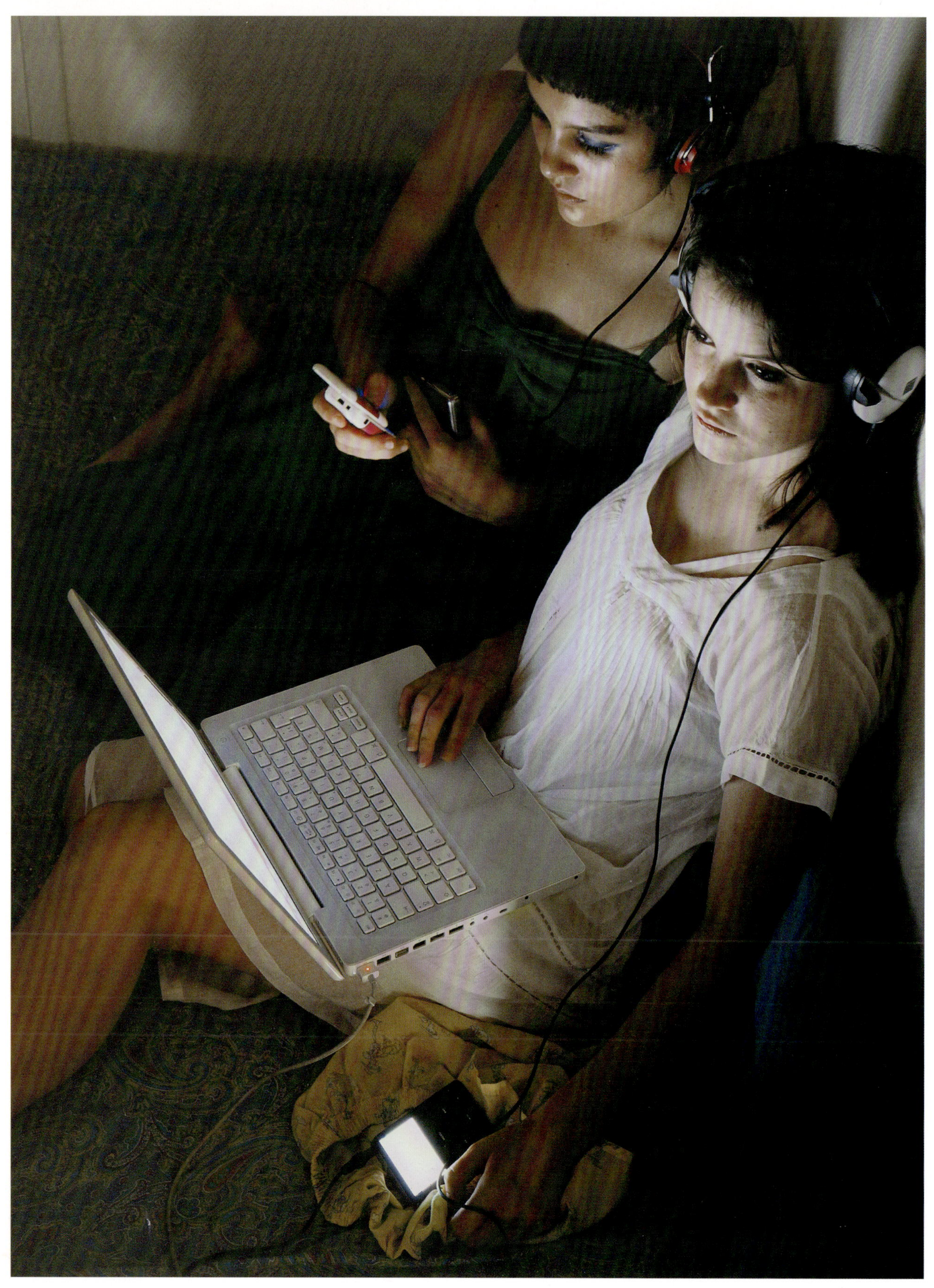

CATHERINE BALET
INES CONNECTED WITH AMINA
FROM THE SERIES *CONNECTED*
JUNE 2008

THIRD PRIZE
CATHERINE BALET

A chance observation on a train gave French photographer Catherine Balet the raw idea for her entry, *Ines Connected with Amina*. Travelling in the UK, Balet was struck by the number of young women immersed in their mobile phones and MP3 players. 'There was one woman wearing huge earphones pouring over a BlackBerry – a typically busy young Englishwoman of today,' she recalls. 'She got off the train and hurried away before I had the opportunity to approach her, but she gave me the idea of recreating a similar set-up.'

Enlisting her best friend's daughter, Ines, and fellow teen, Amina, Balet staged an equivalent scene in Ines's bedroom in Paris, with the subjects lit only by the glare of their technology and a TV in the corner of the room. 'It was a quick process. In fact, I woke up that morning with the vision of the scene. I told the girls where and how to sit and then to be themselves until it seemed right. It worked out better than I could have imagined.' Though she usually works with a 4x5 large format camera in negative, the picture was taken with a digital Canon EOS 5D. 'As the subject was about connection in a digital world, I wanted it to have that digital touch.'

Balet was born in 1959, studied at the École des Beaux Arts in Paris and worked as an artist before turning to photography ten years ago. As a freelancer, she is now a regular contributor to various French fashion magazines. 'Painting is about introspection and I became bored of looking inside,' she says. 'So much is going on outside and so fast. Photography is a wonderful way to discover places that you wouldn't have otherwise seen.'

A great deal of Balet's work centres on youth culture. In 2006 she published *Identity*, a collection of pictures that explored the 'tribal subdivisions of the adolescent fashion world'. In a similar vein, her portrait of Ines and Amina is the first image in a new project, *Connected*, that is set to depict the rise of social networking and what Balet describes as the 'globalisation of intimacy'.

'I am forty-eight years old, but still feel like a teenager in my head. Young people are the future. They are in this transformation period where everything is possible. What I am looking for in photography is this moment, close to ecstasy, when the framing, the light and the expression of the subject get near to what feels like perfection and a little something magical appears. My favourite activity is looking at people, looking again, and trying to depict what's special, what's new, and thinking about what I can say.'

INTERVIEW BY RICHARD MCCLURE

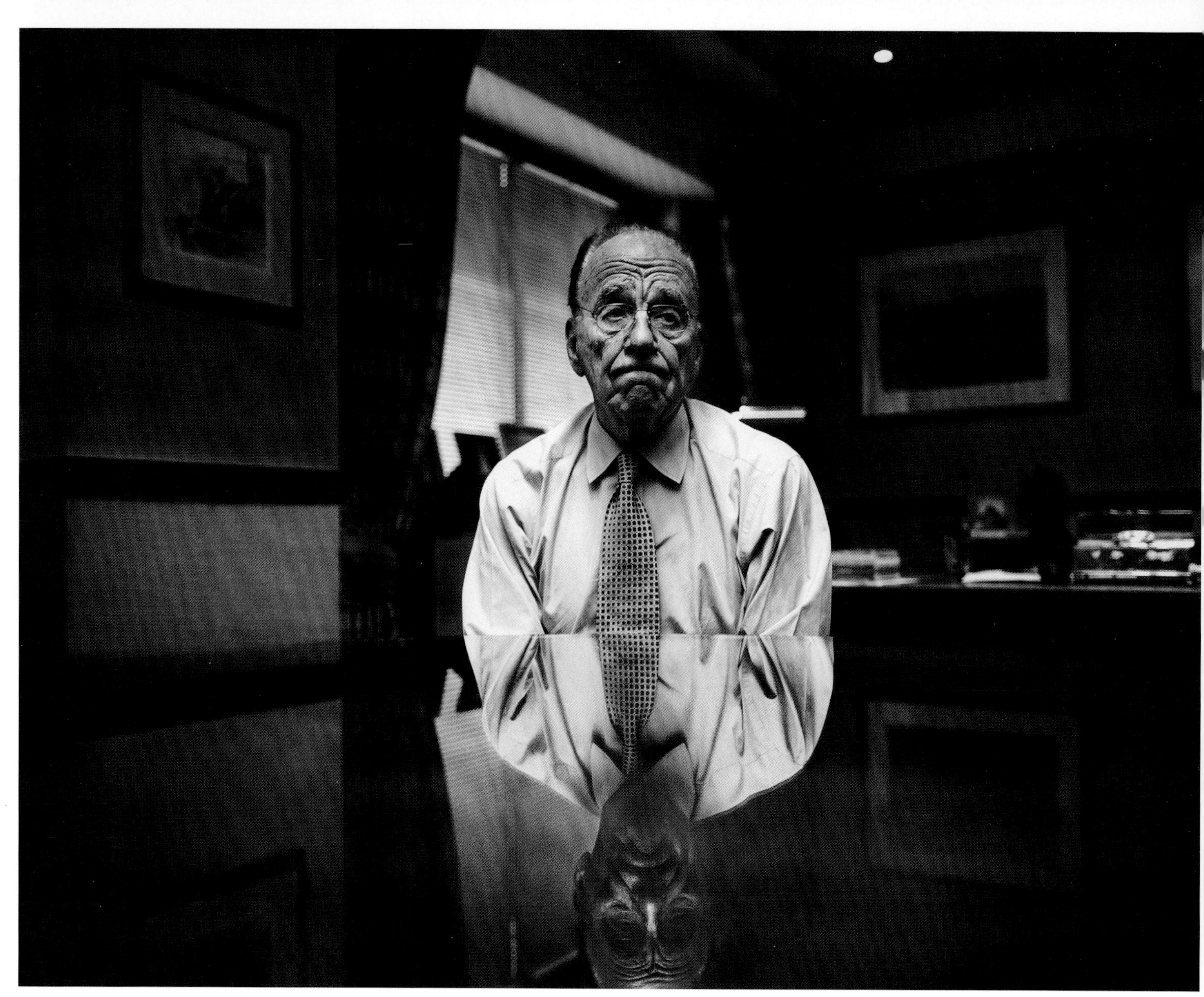

TOM STODDART
MURDOCH REFLECTS
MAY 2007

FOURTH PRIZE
TOM STODDART

From humble beginnings as a teenage apprentice on a local newspaper in his native north-east England, Tom Stoddart has become one of the world's most respected photojournalists, receiving worldwide acclaim for his humanitarian images from war zones in Lebanon, the Balkans and Iraq. A self-described 'journalist of attachment', his latest work bears witness to the catastrophic Aids pandemic in Africa and the war on terror in Afghanistan and Pakistan. 'I shoot my best pictures when I'm angry about something,' he says. 'It is possible for a photographer to remain neutral and objective, but that isn't the way I work.'

In 1997 Stoddart was given exclusive behind-the-scenes access to Tony Blair's election campaign as Labour swept to victory, and he has continued to prowl the corridors of power, 'hunting images' of movers and shakers in a range of photo essays. His entry, *Murdoch Reflects*, is taken from an assignment for *Time* magazine and shows media mogul Rupert Murdoch at his News Corporation offices in London. Stoddart spent five days shadowing the Australian businessman as he completed the $5 billion purchase of Dow Jones & Company.

'Murdoch has an amazing face and is a fascinating character for a photographer,' he says. 'He doesn't give that kind of access very often so it was strange for him when he realised I wasn't going away. There were a couple of times when I felt invisible and he didn't really know or care that I was there and this image comes from one of those moments. I liked the picture as soon I saw it. The reflection on the desk makes it an interesting visual shape, and it's not often that you see Murdoch looking quite so small and vulnerable.'

Despite the advent of digital technology, Stoddart remains a passionate advocate of film, shooting mainly in mono and using short focal length lenses on Leica rangefinders. 'Black-and-white is a very powerful medium and it moves people more than colour,' he says. 'I want the camera to be part of me and feel intimate. I use portraiture a lot in my documentary work because I am trying to see into people's eyes. That's why I work so closely and on very simple equipment.'

When he moved to London in 1978, Stoddart freelanced extensively for the *Sunday Times Magazine* and was injured while on assignment for the publication in 1992, trying to escape sniper fire in Sarajevo. Now represented by Getty Images in order to 'tell my own stories', he has been awarded Nikon Photographer of the Year three times, while his retrospective exhibition, *iWitness*, drew record crowds to the Royal Festival Hall, London, in 2004.

'Every now and again, people say to me that photojournalism is dead. Well, that is blatant nonsense,' he insists. 'Video footage flashes in front of you, and when it's gone, it's gone. But a good still image can imbed itself into your brain. There remains a hell of a need for campaigning photojournalism. It can continue to be the tool to inform and move people, which is what it's all about.'

INTERVIEW BY RICHARD MCCLURE

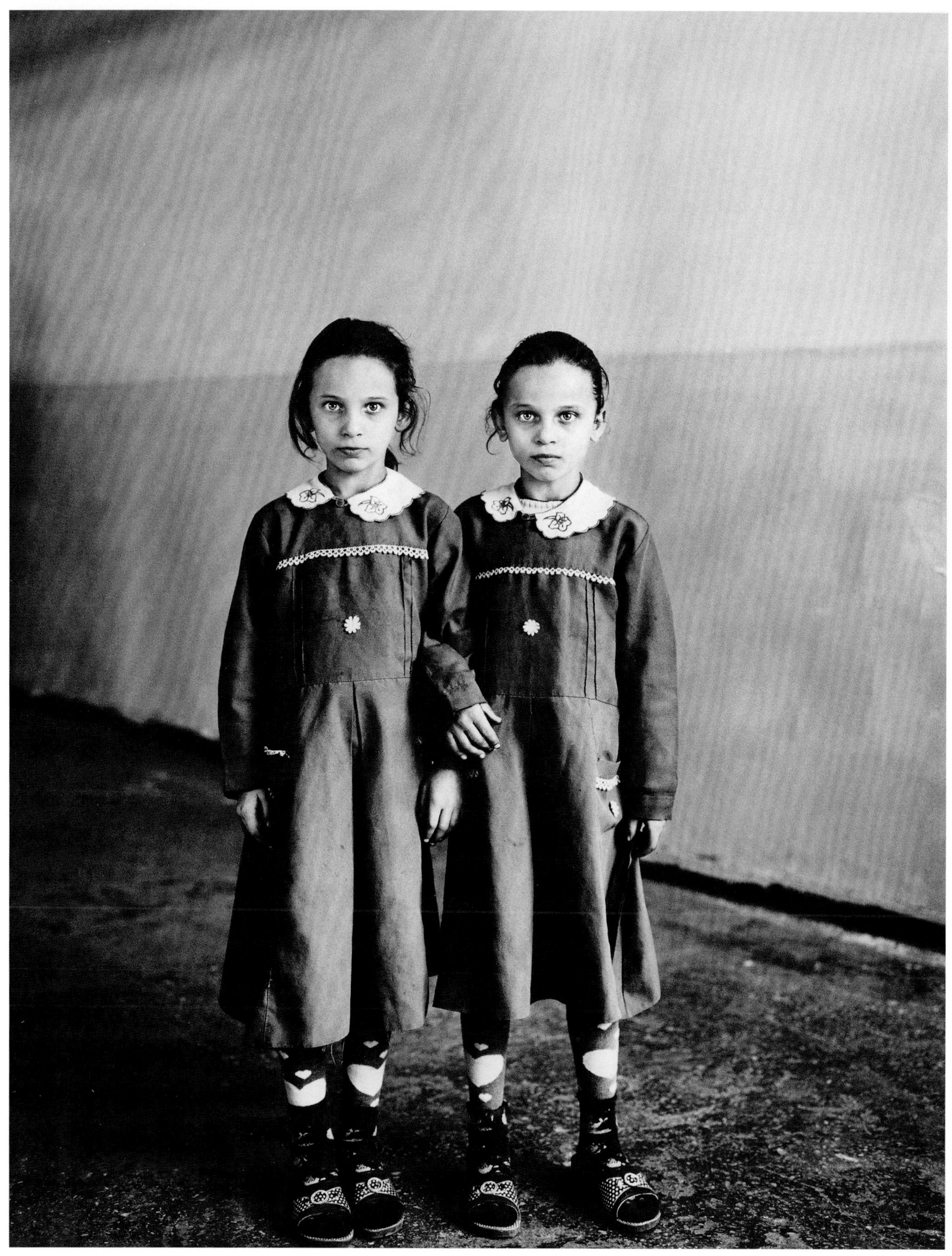

VANESSA WINSHIP
SWEET NOTHINGS
FROM THE SERIES *SWEET NOTHINGS*
OCTOBER 2007

14

GODFREY ARGENT AWARD
VANESSA WINSHIP

Recipient of the Godfrey Argent Award for the best black-and-white portrait, Vanessa Winship has recently returned to the UK after living and working in Turkey for several years. Her winning entry, *Sweet Nothings*, was taken in the East Anatolia region of the country and comes from a series of portraits inspired by a government campaign to educate rural girls.

'One enduring image that had always struck me wherever I travelled in Turkey was the schoolgirls in their little blue dresses, the same in every town or village,' she explains. 'Attitudes about educating girls are complex. Until very recently, many girls in the more rural regions had never stepped over the doorstep of a school.'

Winship visited a dozen schools, producing forty-five images of girls posing with their sisters or closest friends. In April she was named 2008 Sony Photographer of the Year for the series, which is also entitled *Sweet Nothings*, a reference to one of the embroidered messages on the girls' uniforms. 'Quite often the uniforms have little messages written in English, which say things like "Flower of Love" or "Love Letter", so there is a strange juxtaposition of these lace collars and sweet words embroidered on what is essentially a symbol of the Turkish state.'

Born in 1960, Winship's own childhood was spent in a 'one horse town' in Lincolnshire where she developed an 'obsessive interest' in old black-and-white pictures of her family. That youthful fascination with mono continues in her own projects, which are exclusively black and white. 'For me, it feels strange that people associate black-and-white photography with reality and truth. Yes, I am trying to be honest in my work, but I am not presenting it as reality. It is very much a two-dimensional representation of my perception of something.'

After gaining a BA in Film, Video and Photographic Arts from the former Polytechnic of Central London, she studied for a post-graduate Diploma in Photojournalism at the former London College of Printing and is now represented by Agence VU. In 2003 she moved to Istanbul from where she documented life in Turkey and neighbouring countries for her first book of reportage, *Black Sea*, published in 2007.

For her schoolgirl portraits she switched from 35mm to a 5x4 plate camera, which requires a long exposure time and gives detailed, high-quality results. 'I wanted to create a space for the girls to have a moment of importance in front of a camera so I used a slower, formal way of making the pictures to create that space,' she explains. 'Many things touched me during the making of the images. I was touched by the gravity in the girls' demeanour, their fragility, their simplicity, their grace, their closeness to one another, but most of all I was struck by their complete lack of posturing.'

INTERVIEW BY RICHARD MCCLURE

THE TAYLOR WESSING PHOTOGRAPHIC PORTRAIT PRIZE
EXHIBITORS

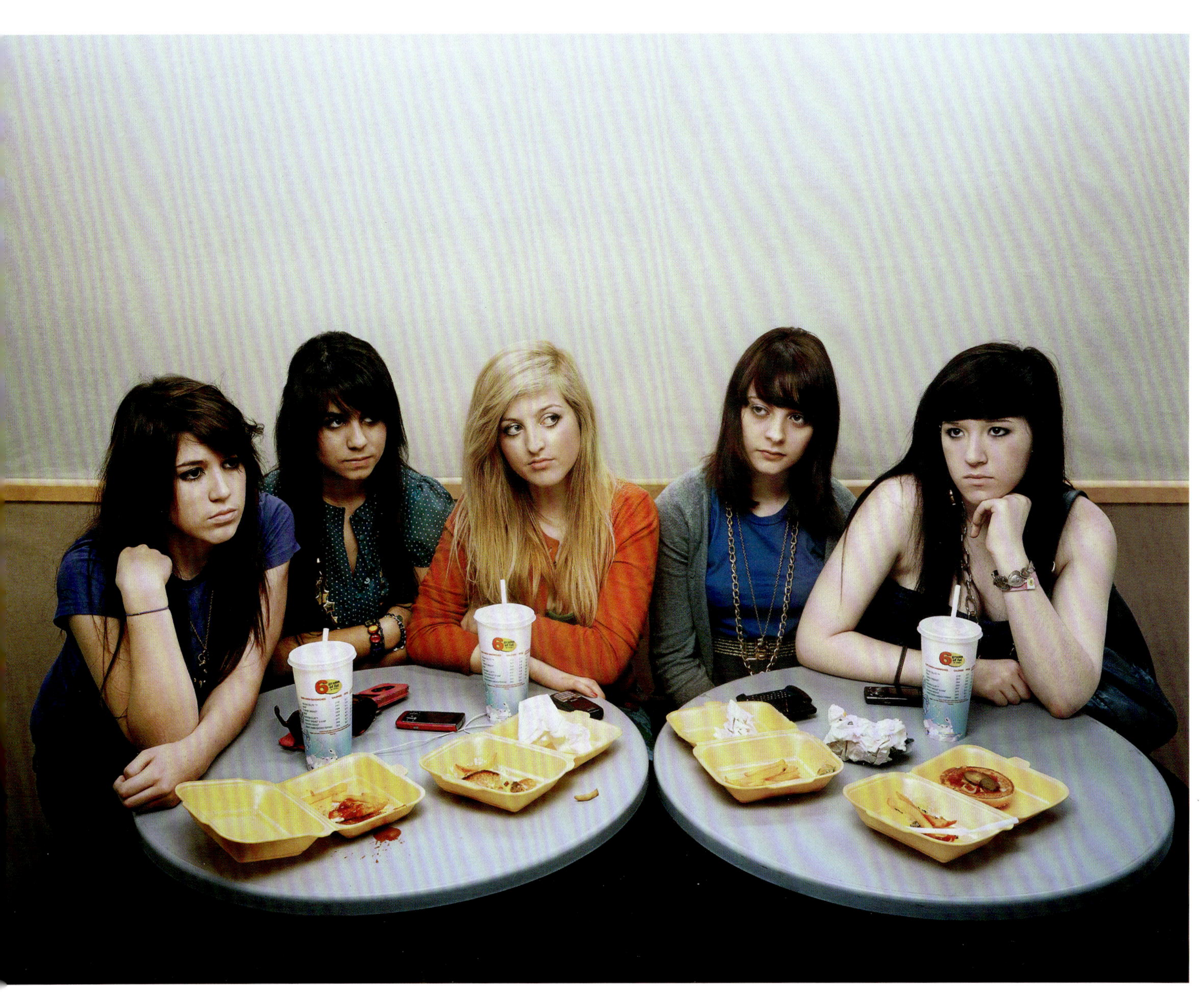

DAVID STEWART
FIVE GIRLS
FROM THE SERIES *RELATIONS*
MAY 2008

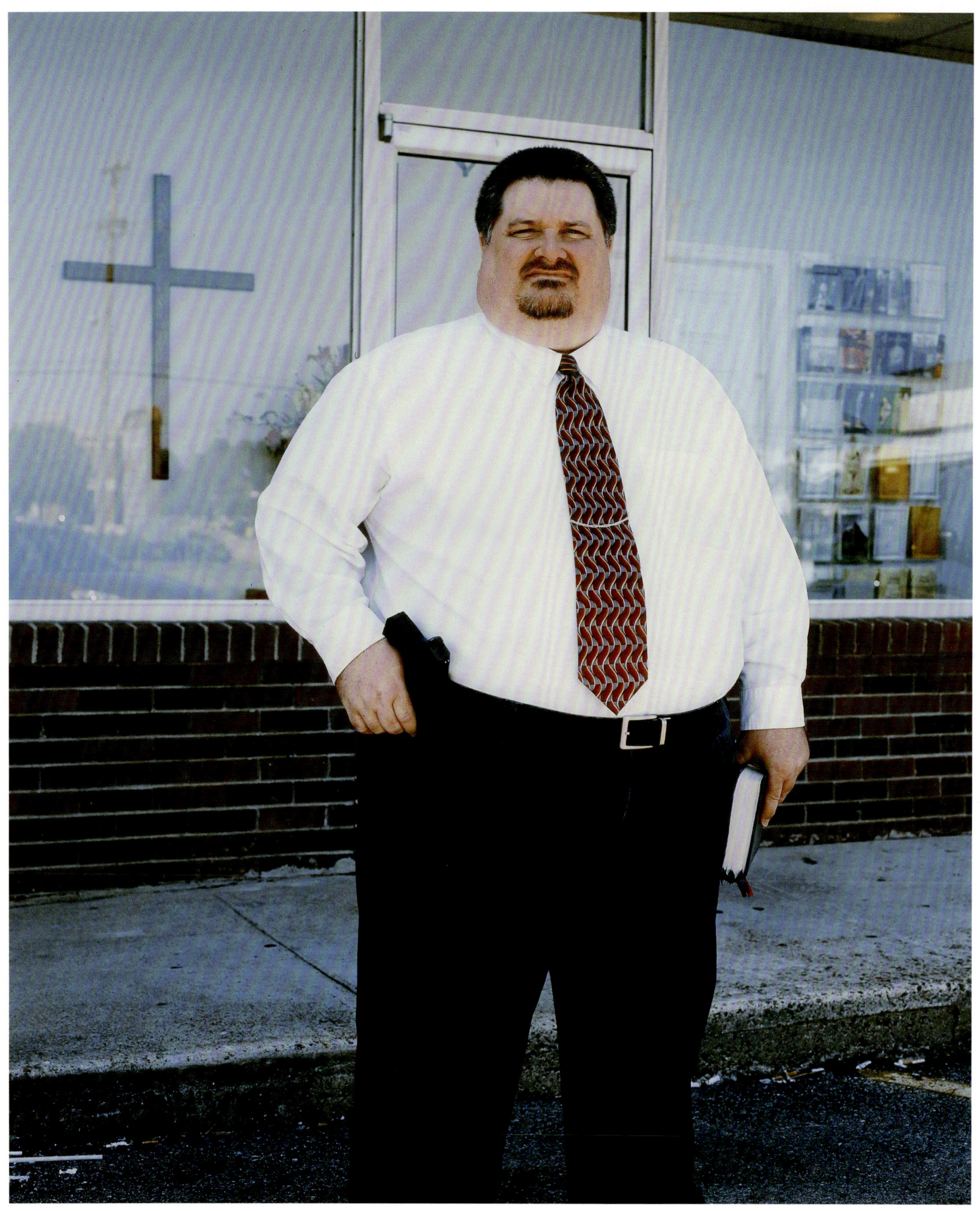

MONICA MEIRA AND MARK JOHNSON
PASTOR PHIL, REFORMED BAPTIST CHURCH, TAURUS PT111
FROM THE SERIES *GOD AND GUNS*
MAY 2008

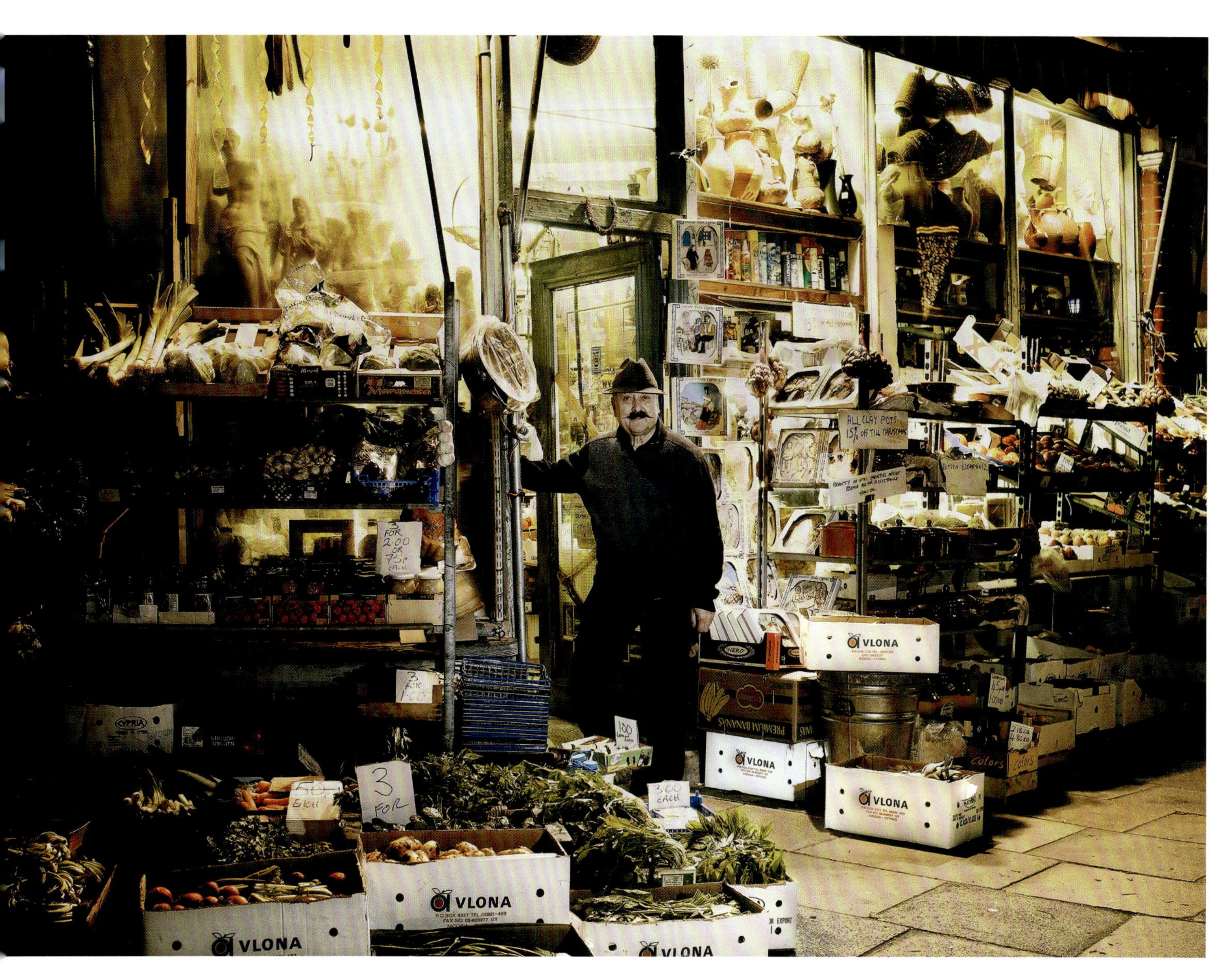

JAMES RUSSELL CANT
ANDREAS
DECEMBER 2007

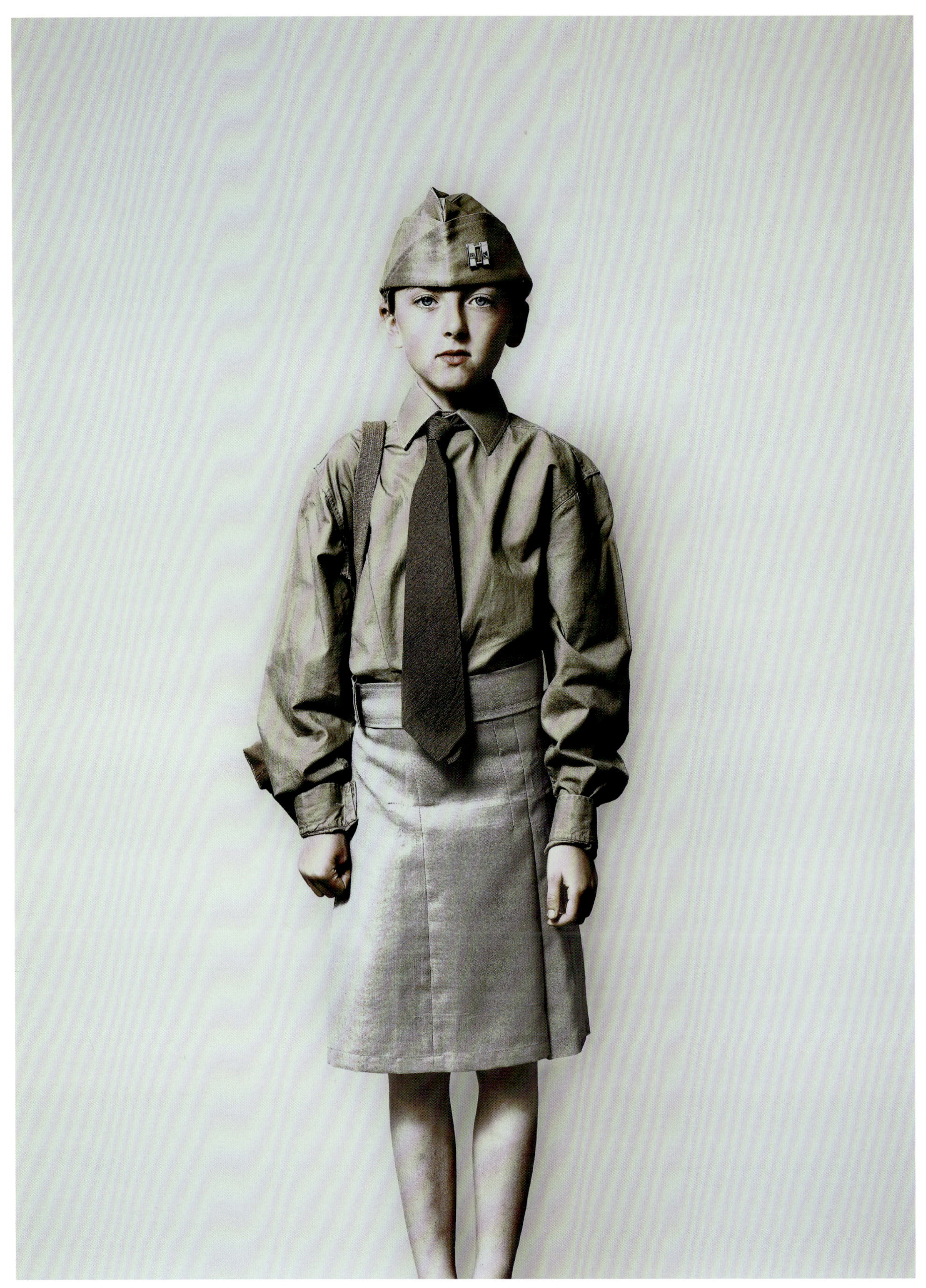

JIM NAUGHTEN
MILITARY RE-ENACTOR 5
AUGUST 2007

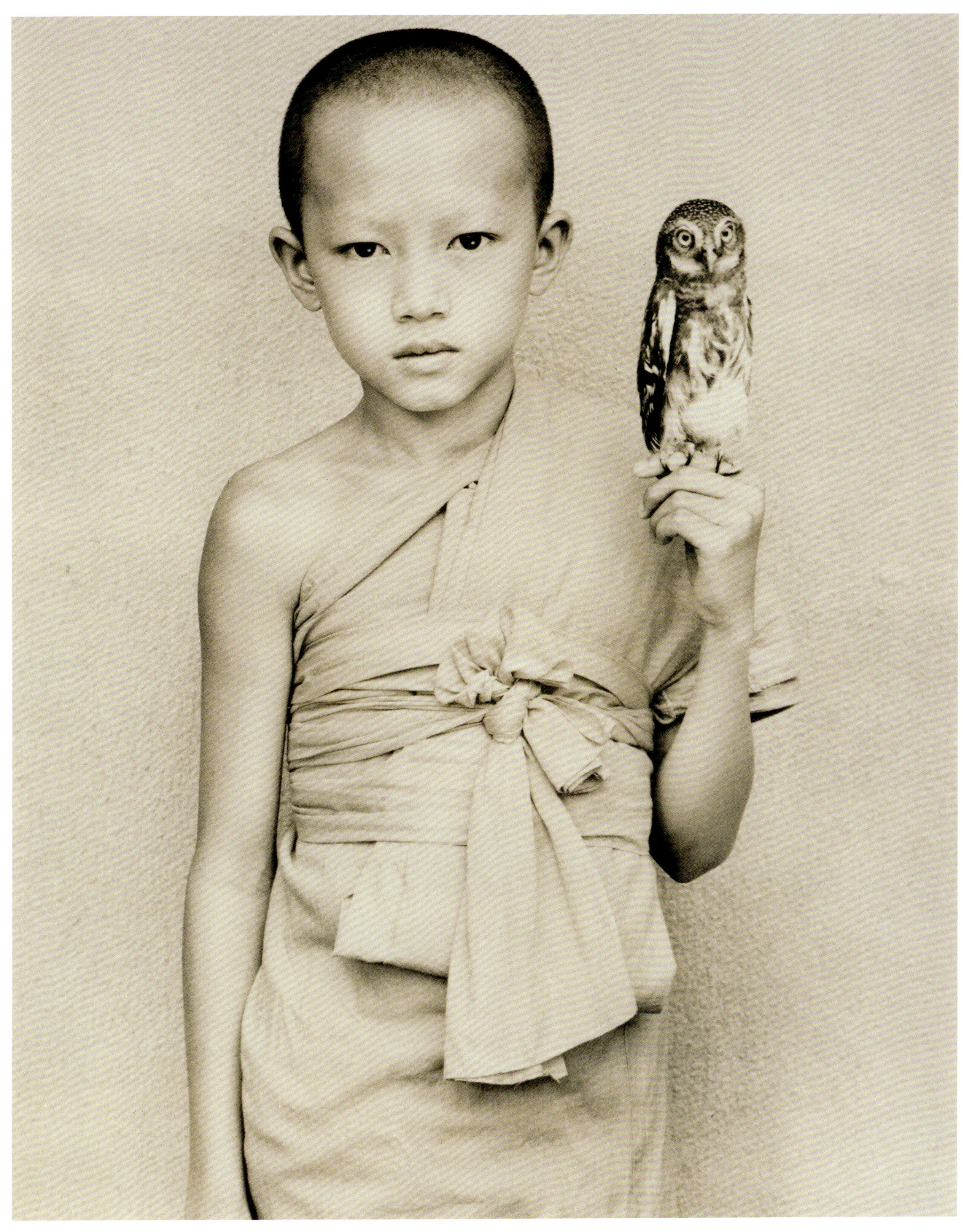

PETER ARNOLD
LITTLE NOVICE
FROM THE SERIES *EAST BY SOUTH-EAST*
FEBRUARY 2007

21

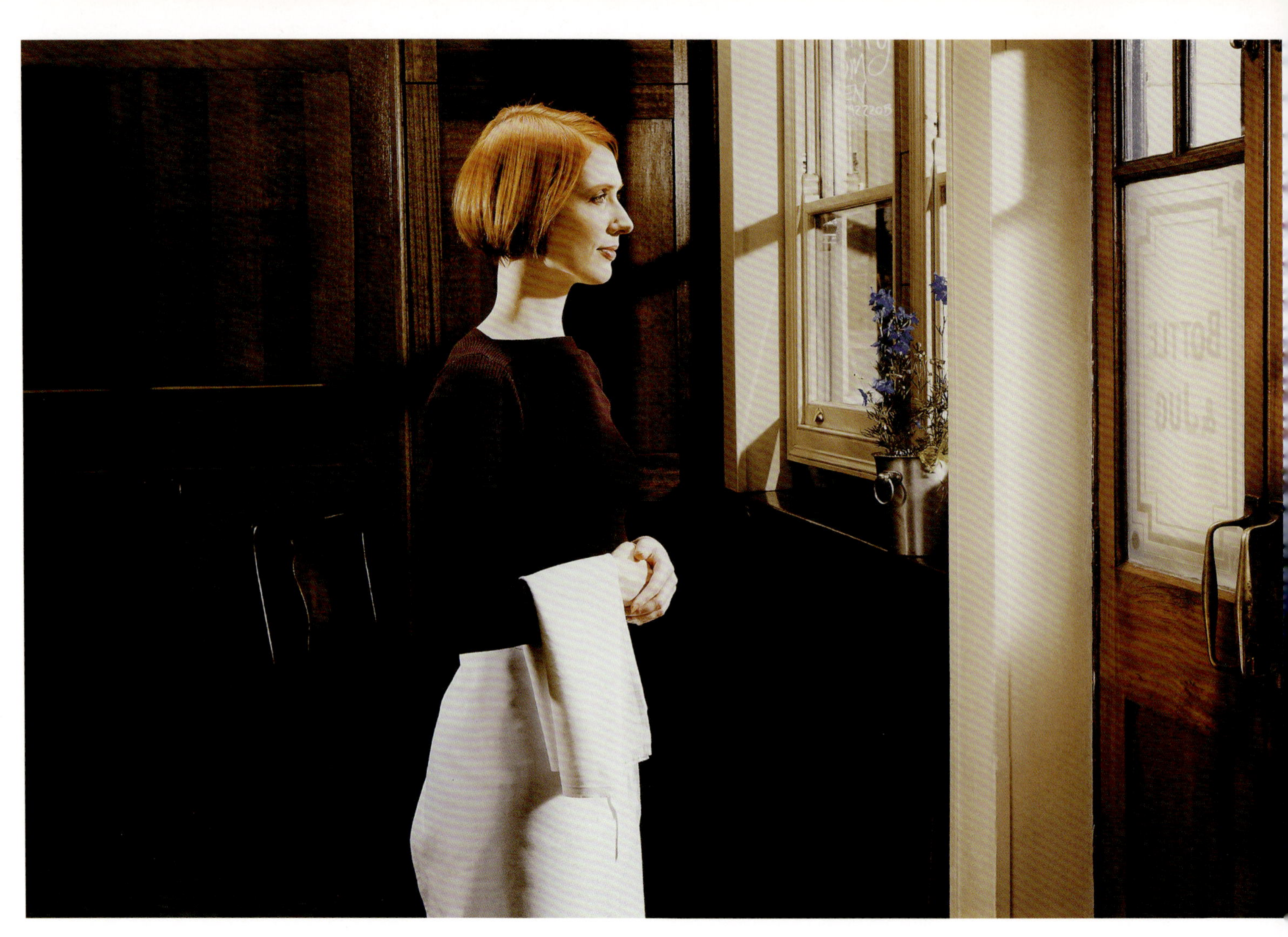

BETSIE VAN DER MEER
WAITRESS
AUGUST 2007

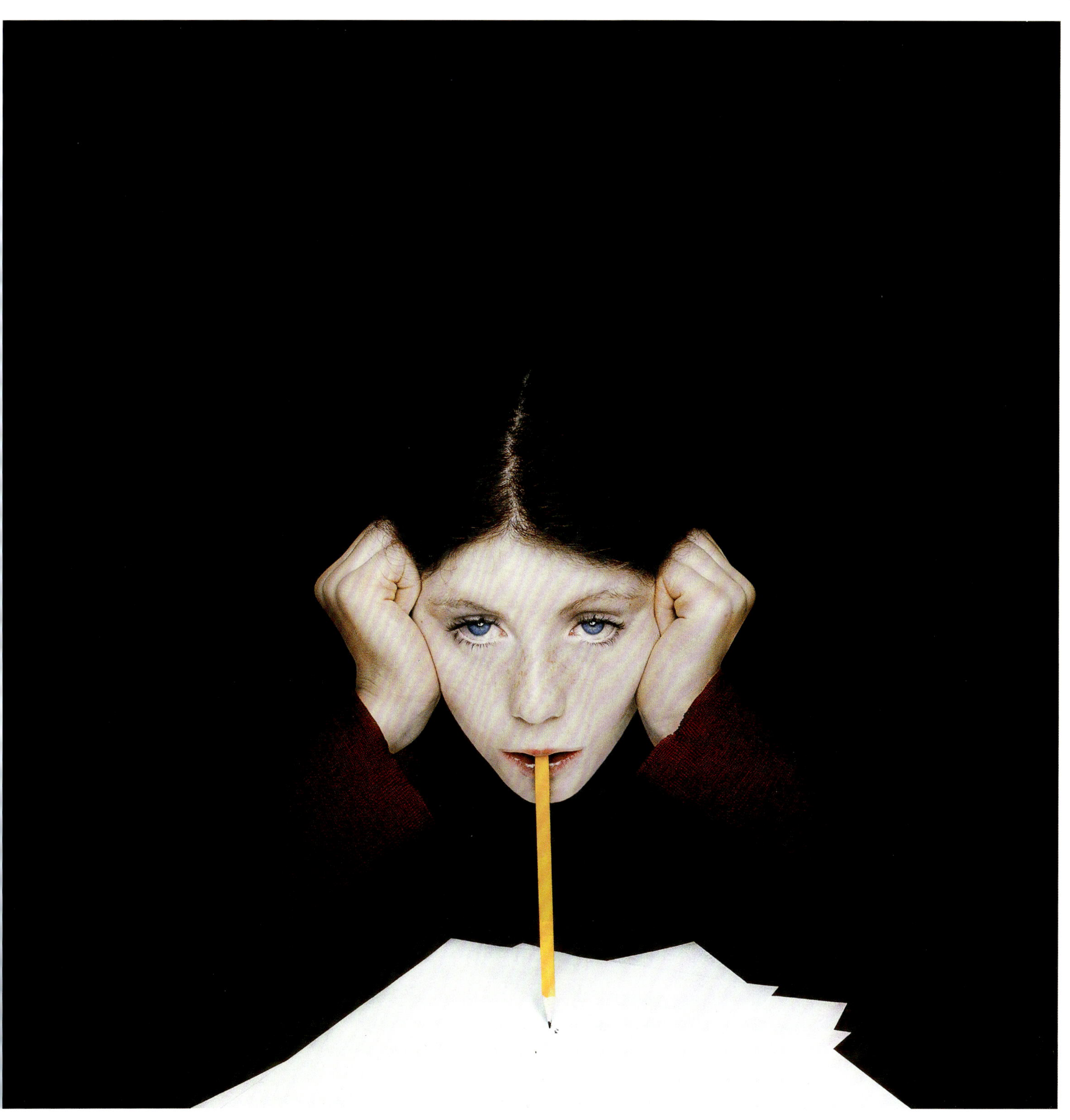

JULIA PEIRONE
SHARPHEAD
SEPTEMBER 2007

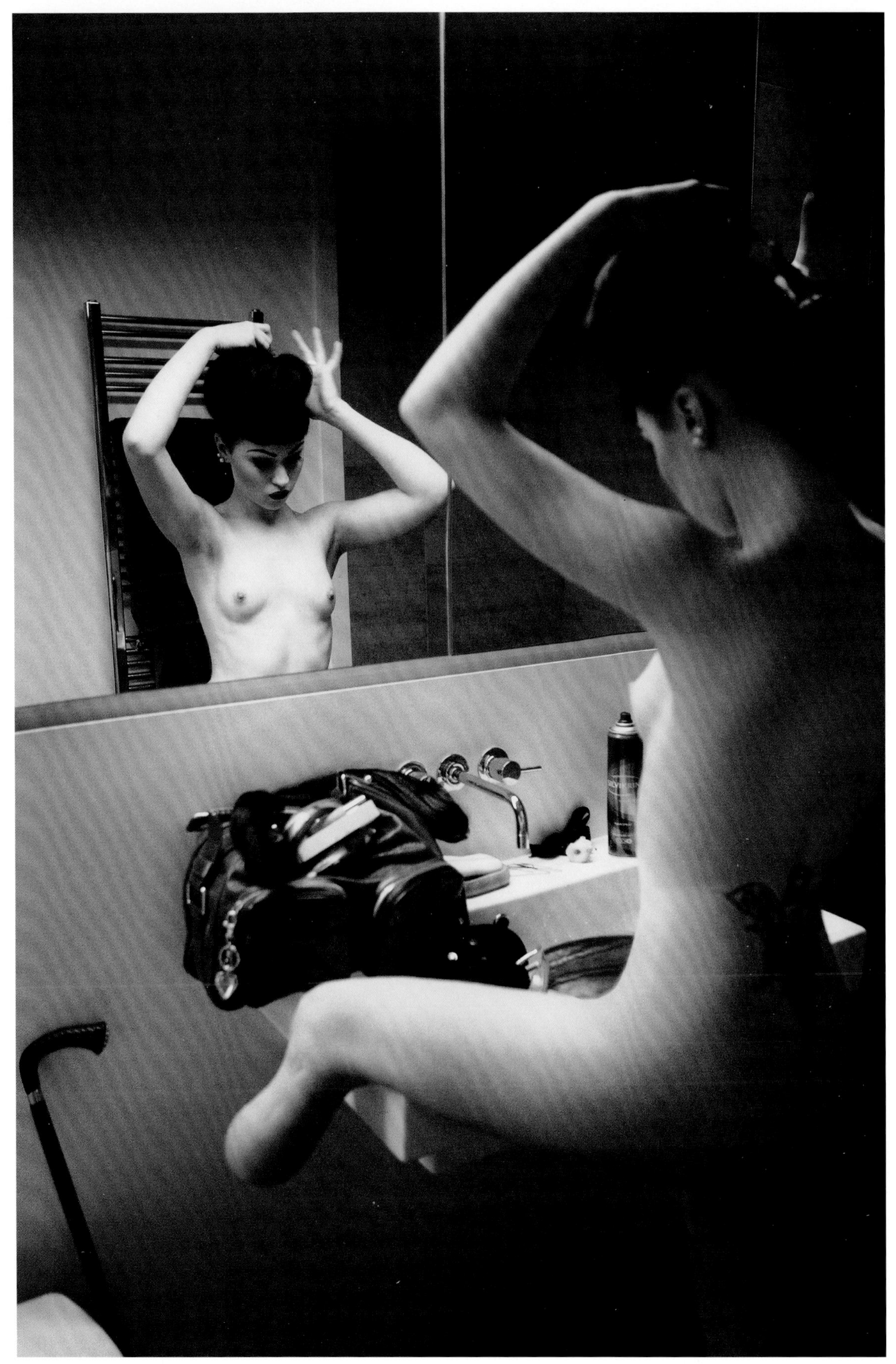

JAMES STROUD

VIKTORIA

FROM THE SERIES *PERSONAL*

OCTOBER 2007

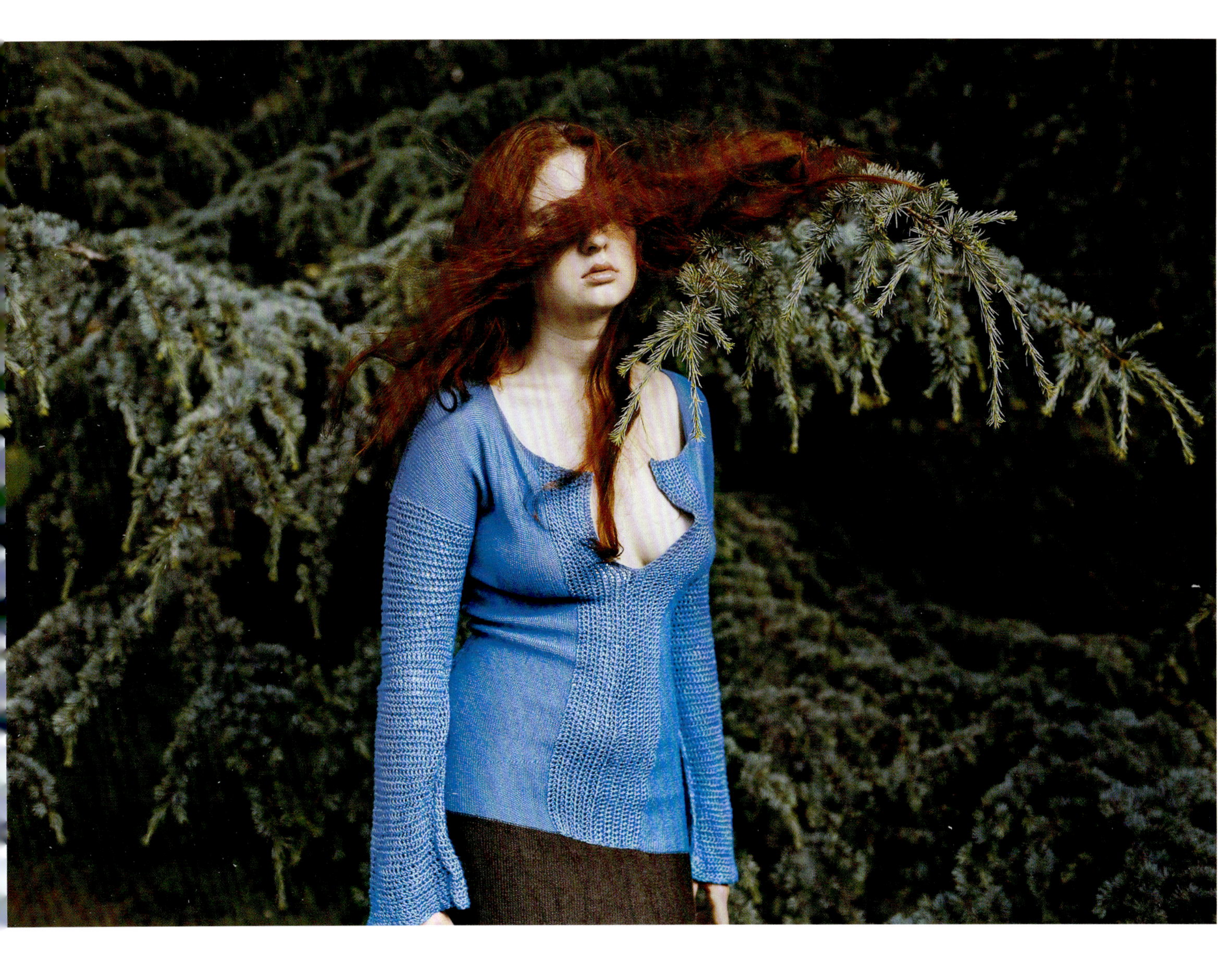

JEAN PASCAL ZAHN
MARINA IN A DRESS BY TINA MIYAKE
FROM THE SERIES *LE RÊVE (THE DREAM)*
JUNE 2008

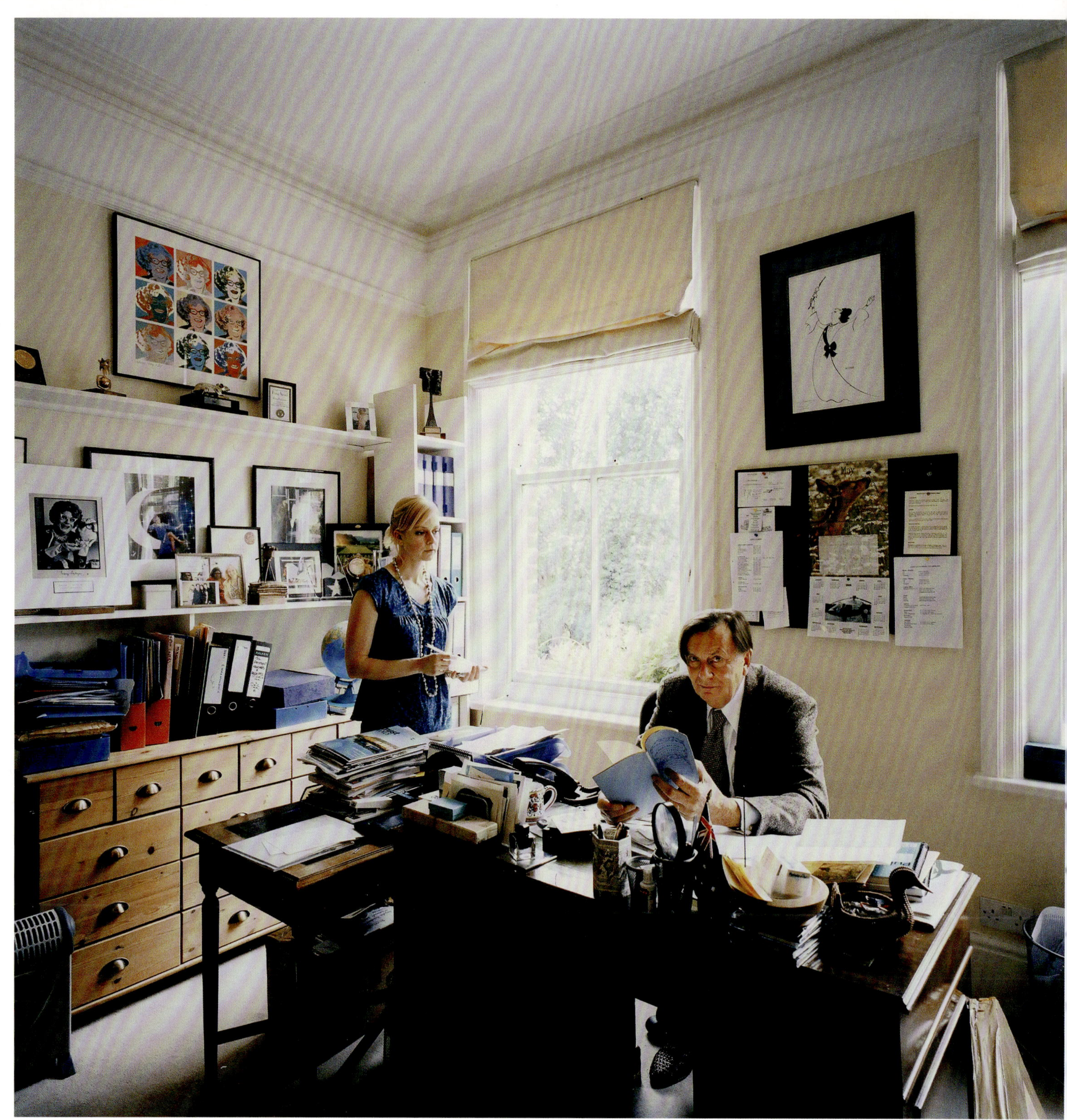

ROBERT PHILLIPS

BARRY HUMPHRIES AND LOLA

JUNE 2008

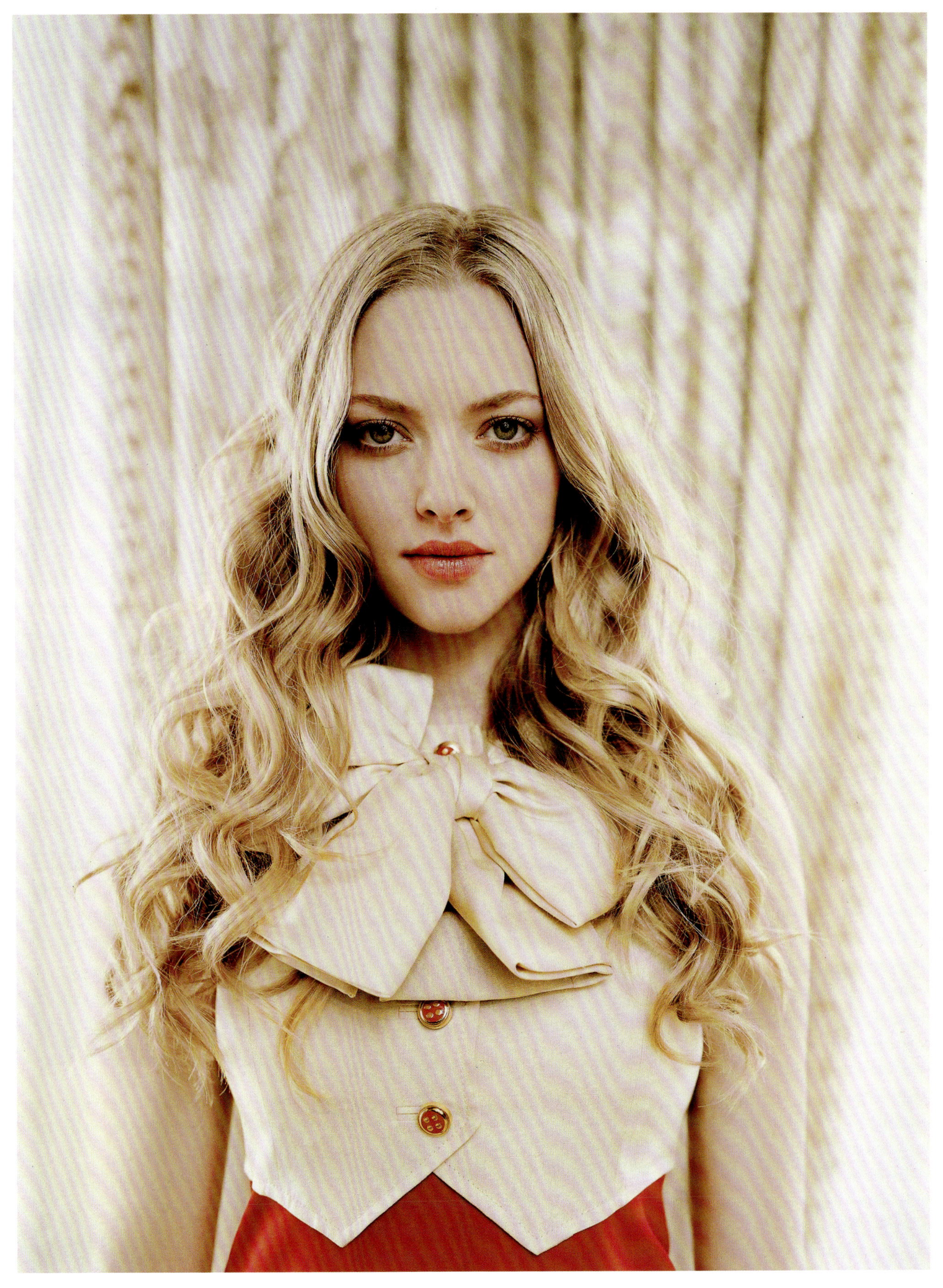

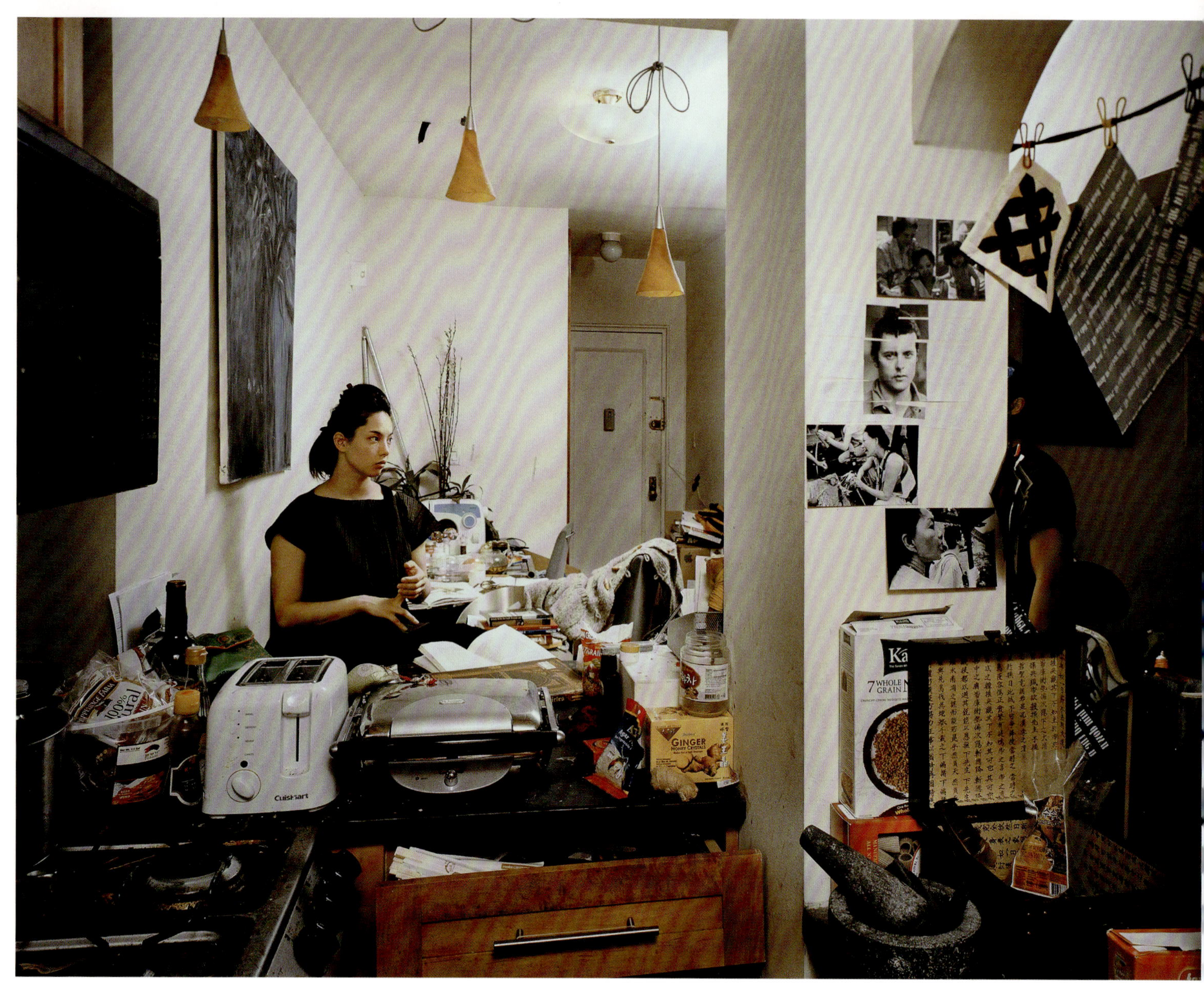

SATOMI SHIRAI

TARA CRONIN
FROM THE SERIES
NEW YORK, WHERE WE MET
MARCH 2008

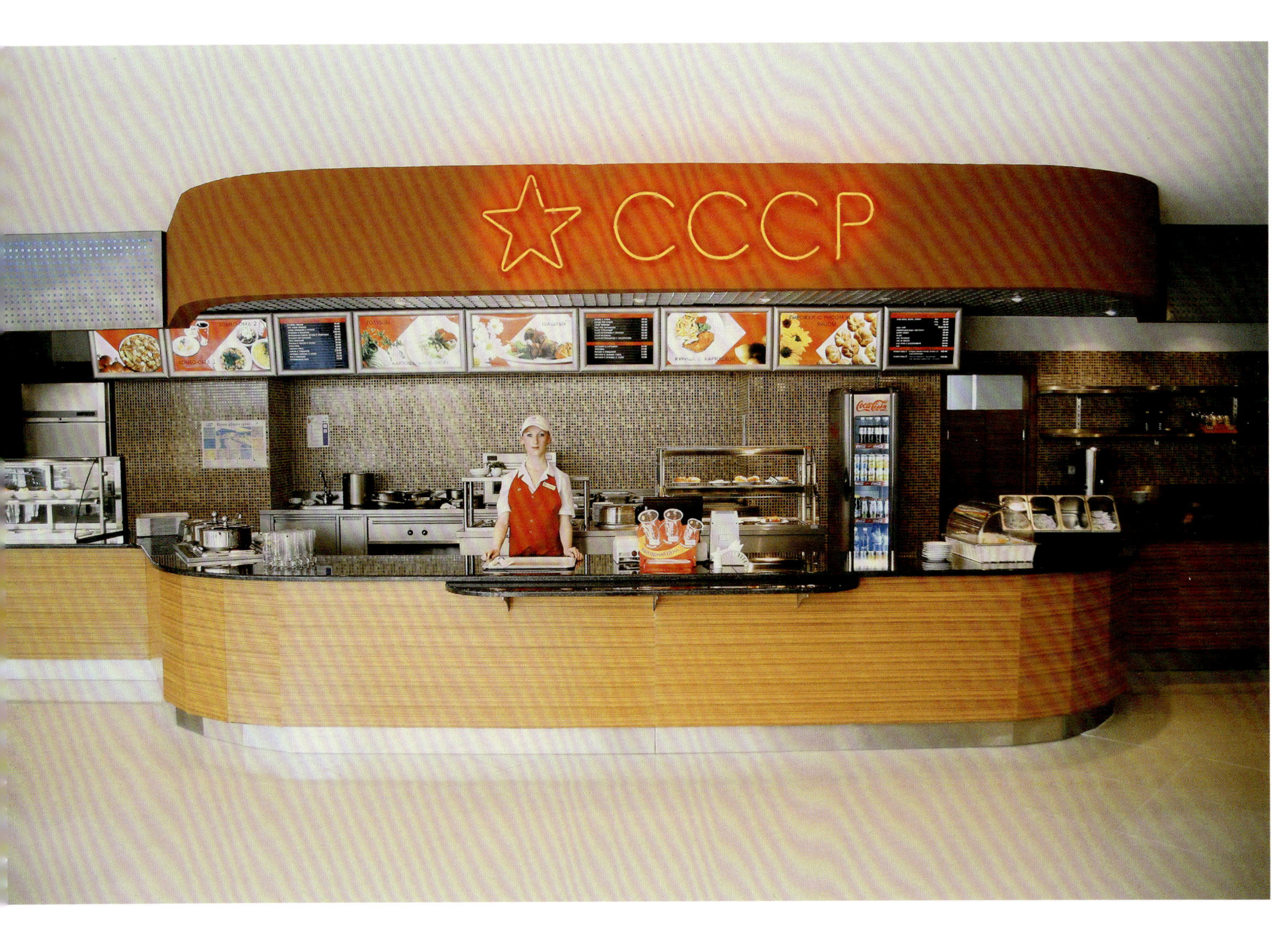

MEREDITH ANDREWS
CCCP
FROM THE SERIES *KAZAN*
MAY 2007

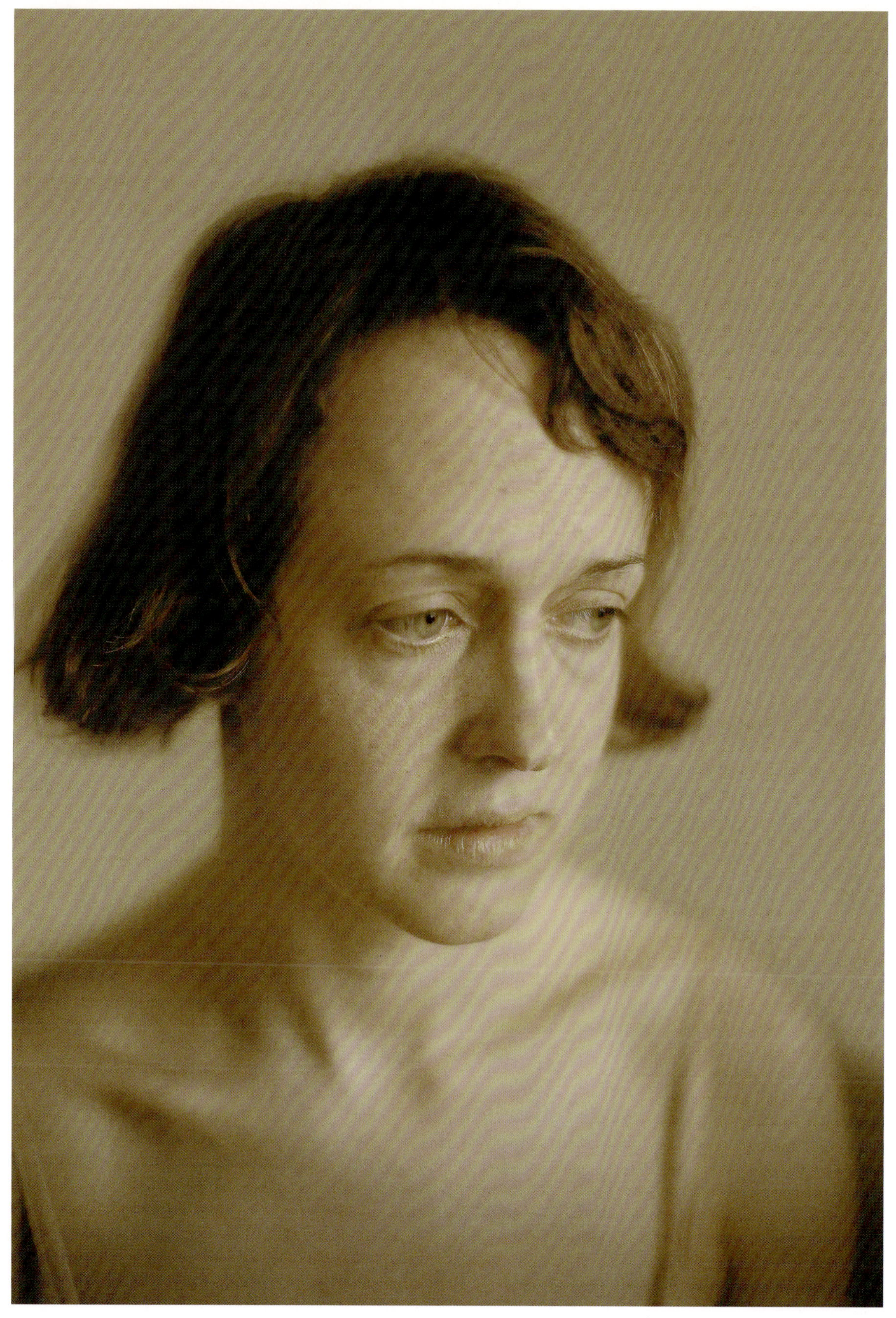

PHOEBE LING
MISS GEE
FROM THE SERIES
AUDEN IN MY PARENTS' SITTING ROOM
APRIL 2008

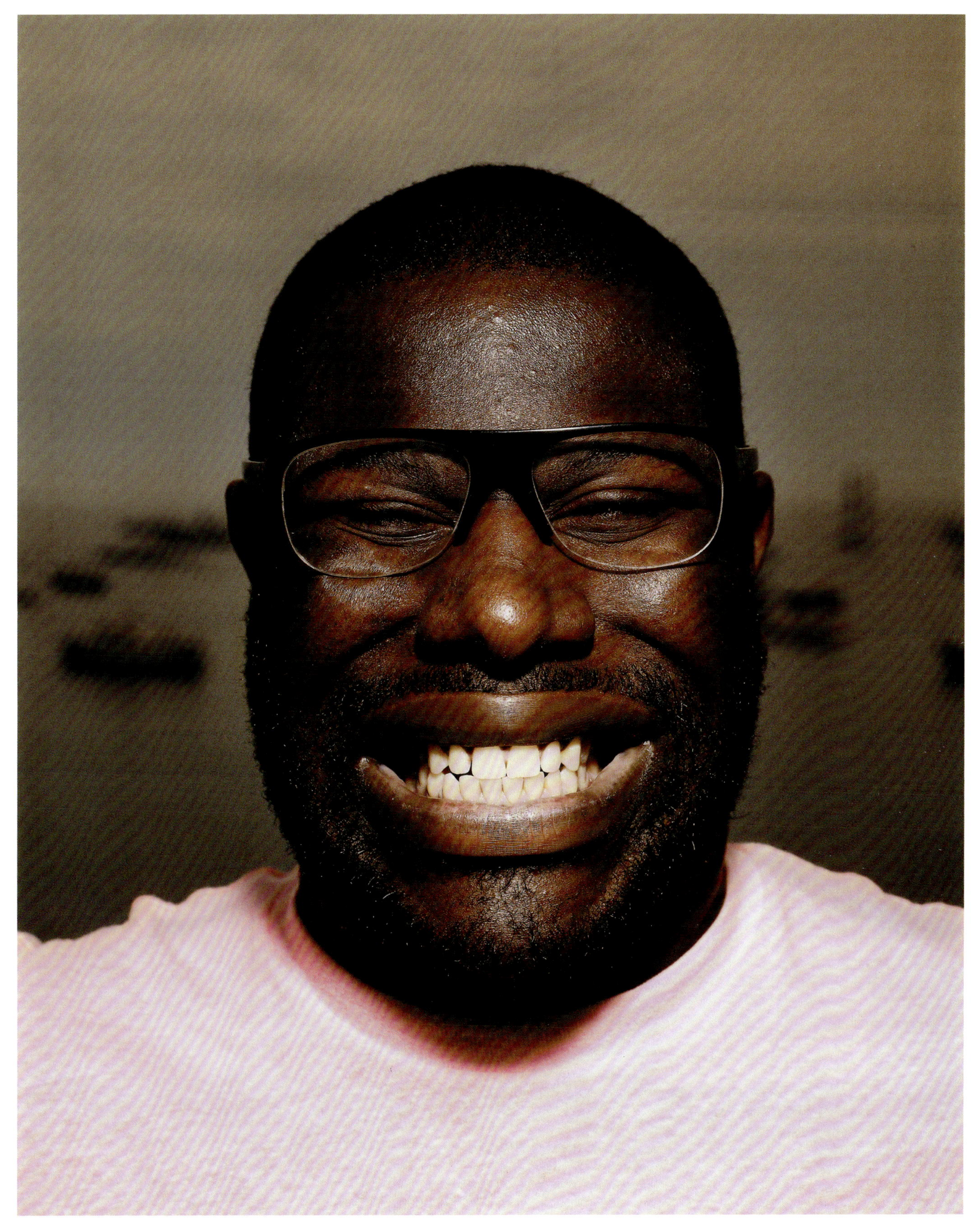

CHRIS FLOYD
STEVE MCQUEEN
MAY 2008

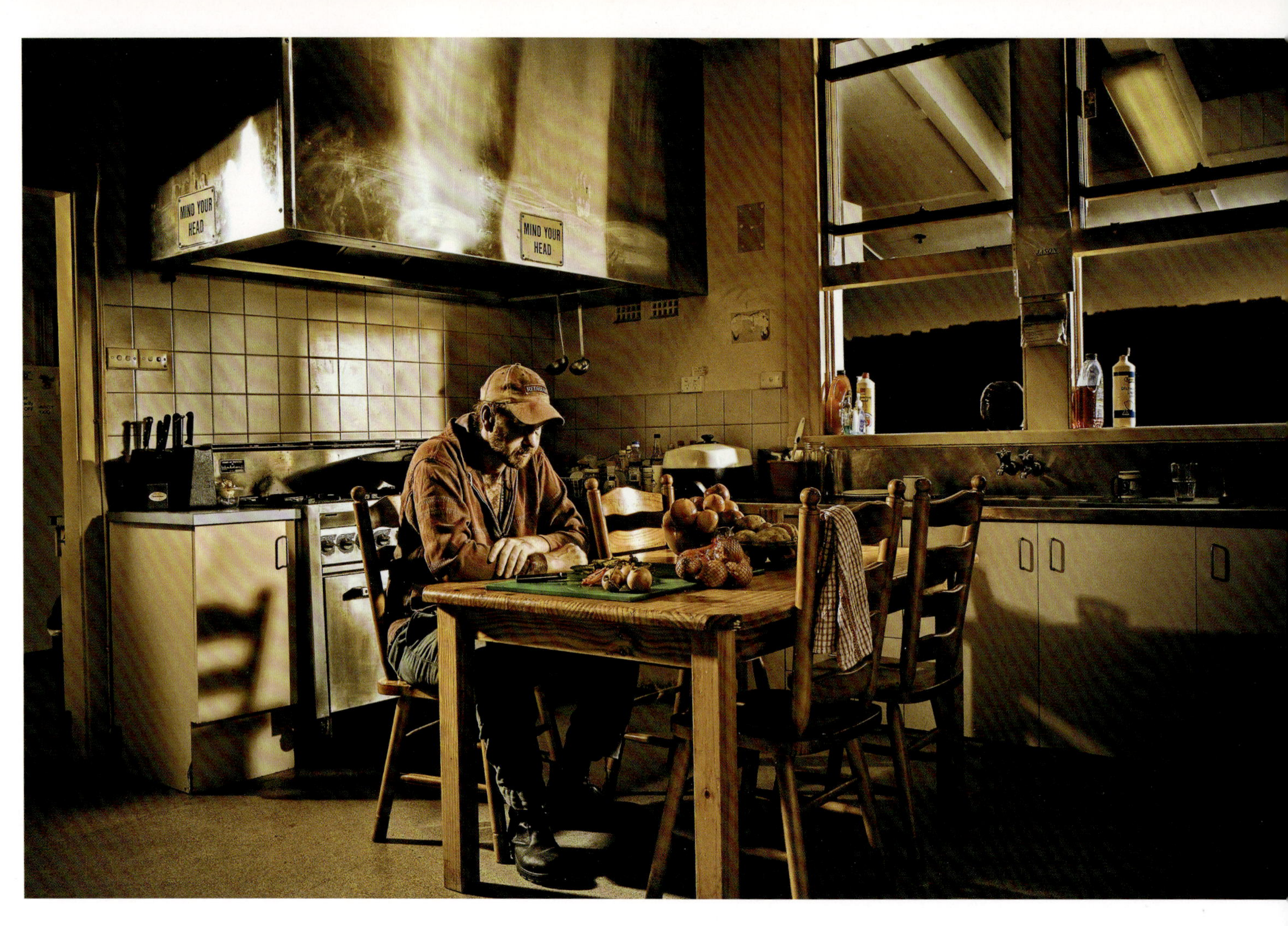

BRONEK KOZKA
BARRY
JULY 2007

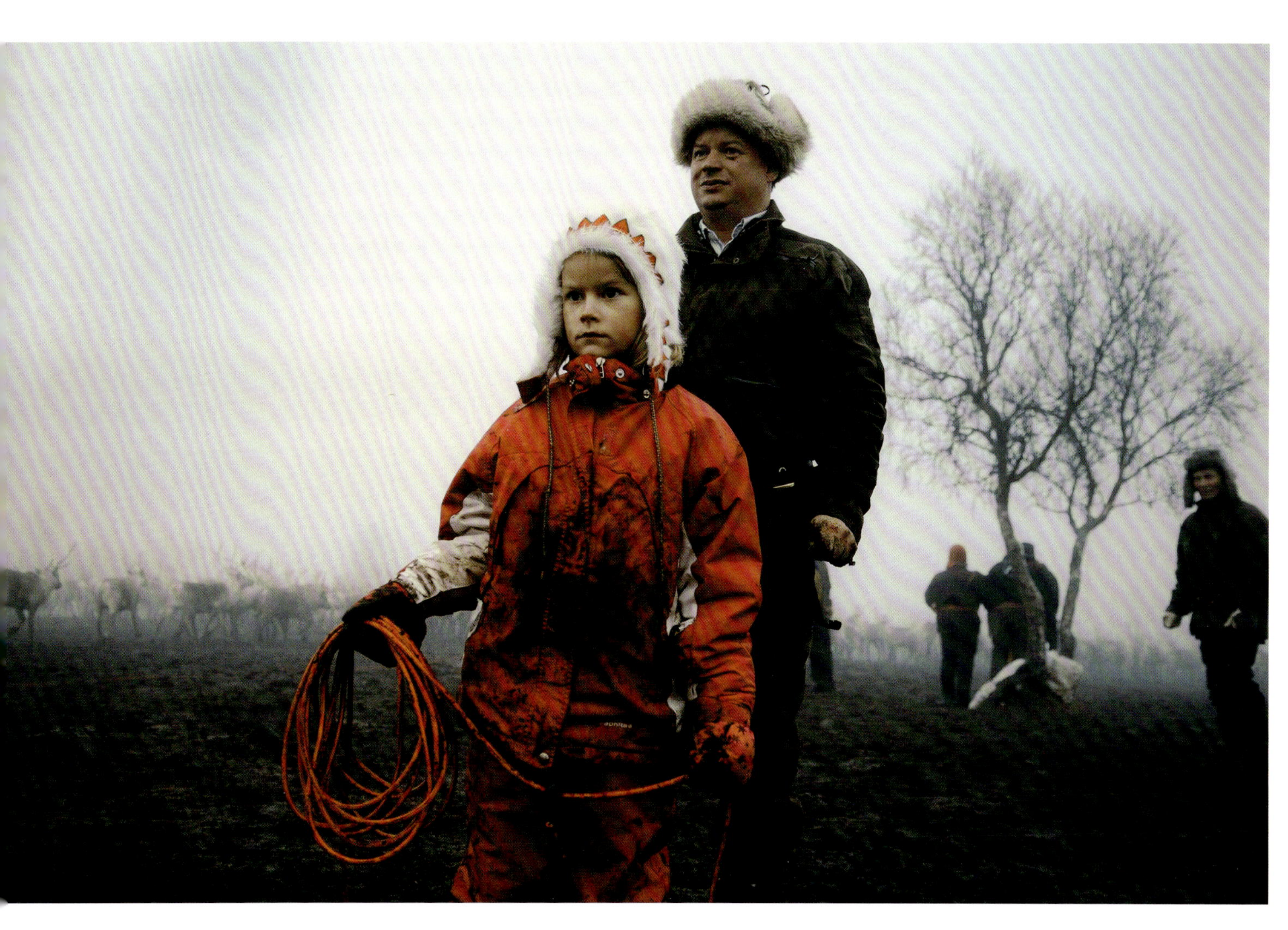

MARK BRYAN MAKELA
FOLLOWING SAMI TRADITION
FROM THE SERIES
SAMI REINDEER HERDERS:
AN ARCTIC TRADITION IMPERILLED
OCTOBER 2007

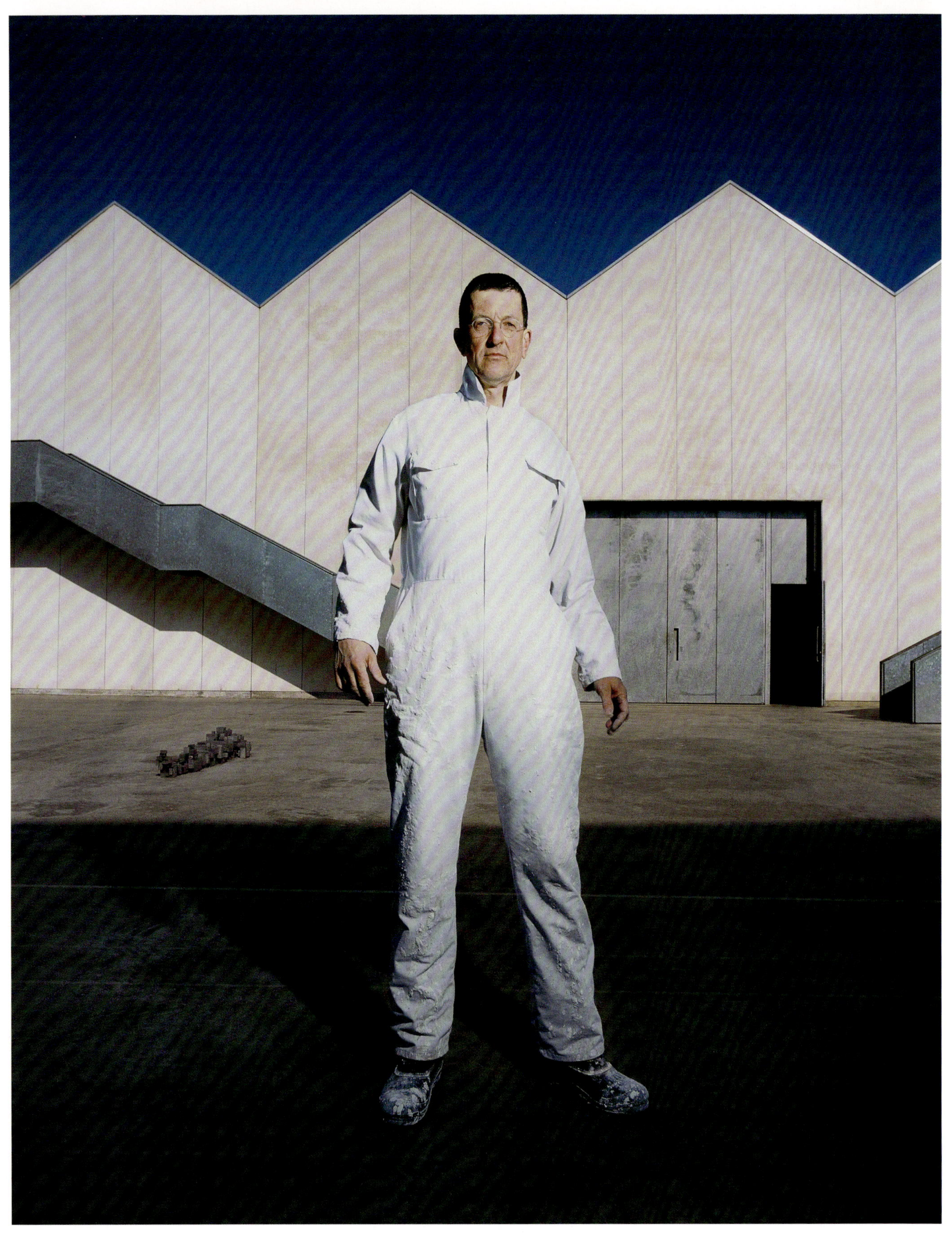

RICHARD ANSETT
ANTONY GORMLEY, LONDON STUDIO
SEPTEMBER 2007

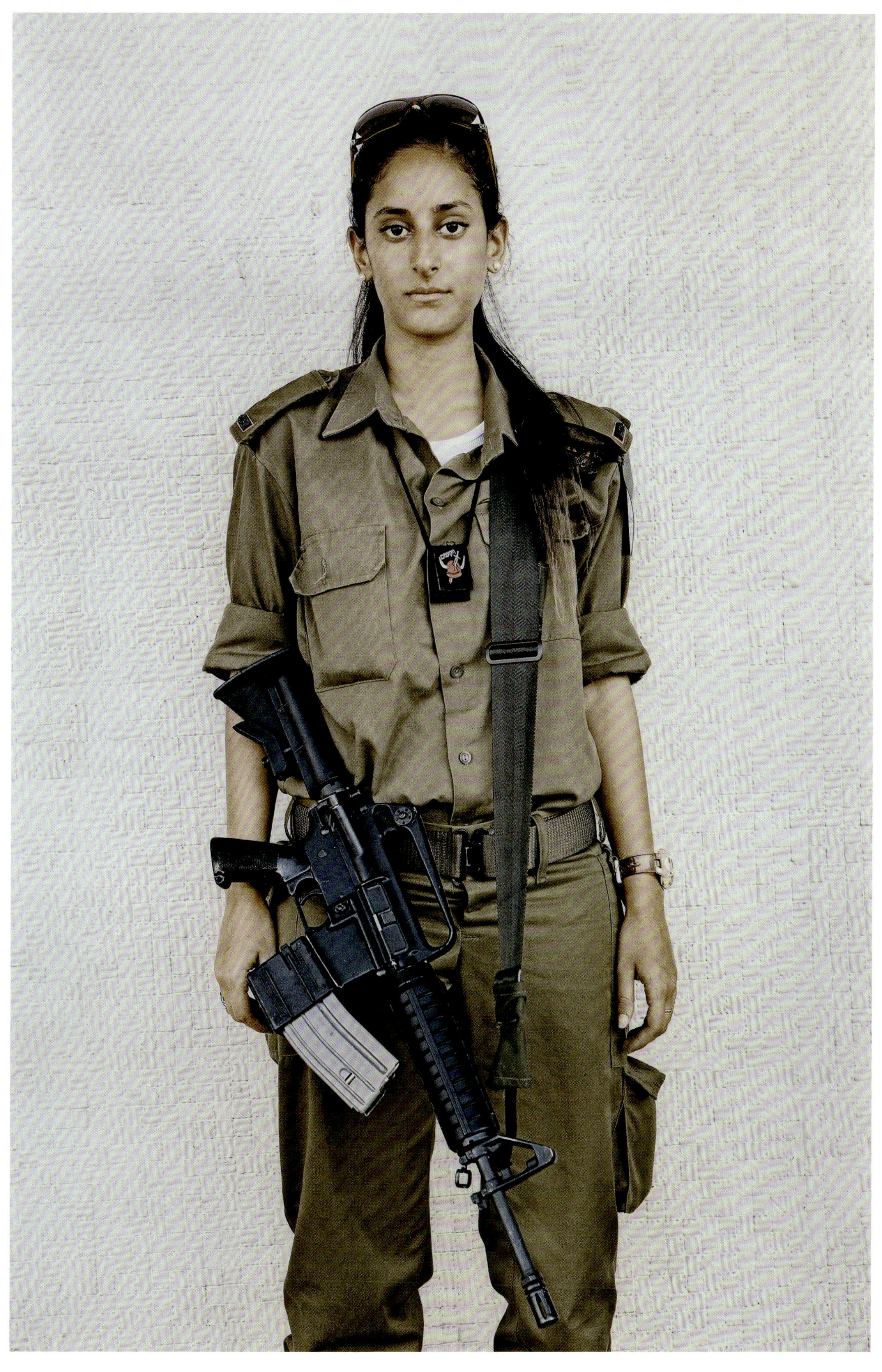

JAMES STROUD
SOLDIER GIRL
FROM THE SERIES YOUNG GUNS
JANUARY 2008

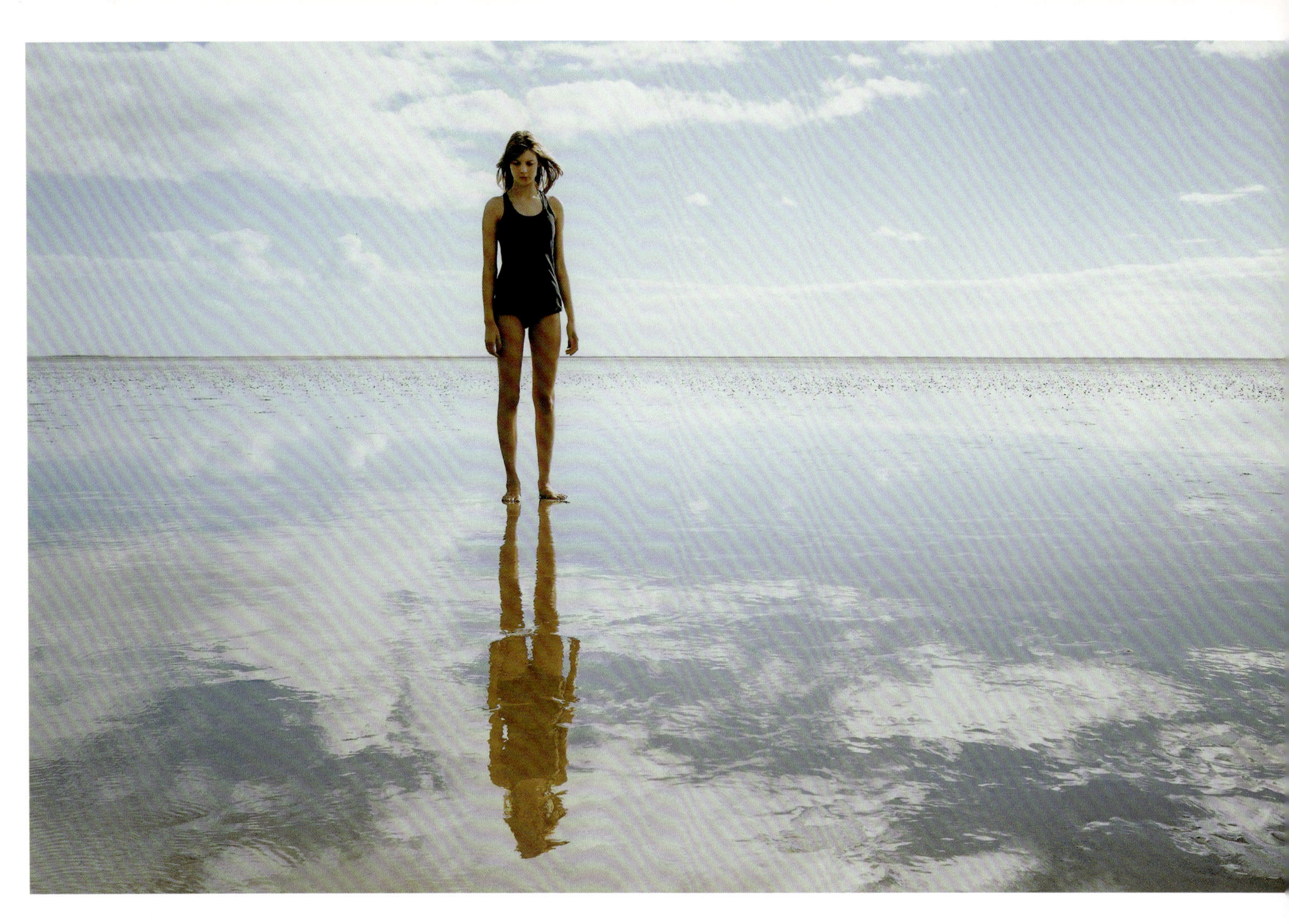

CLARISSA LEAHY
FRANCES – REFLECTION IN WATER
APRIL 2008

36

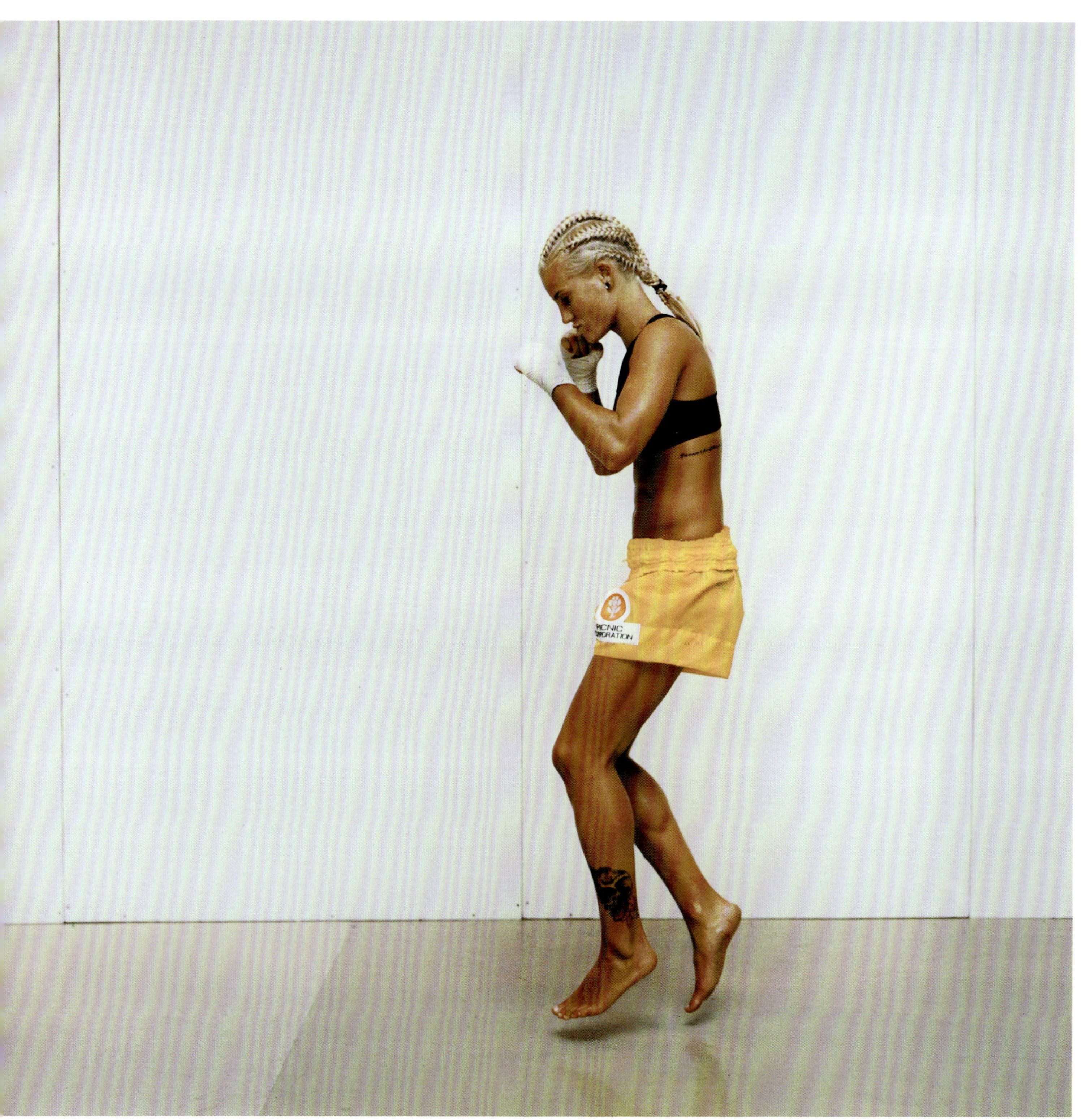

KEITH PRICE
SWEDISH FIGHTER
FROM THE SERIES *WOMEN OF MUAY THAI*
NOVEMBER 2007

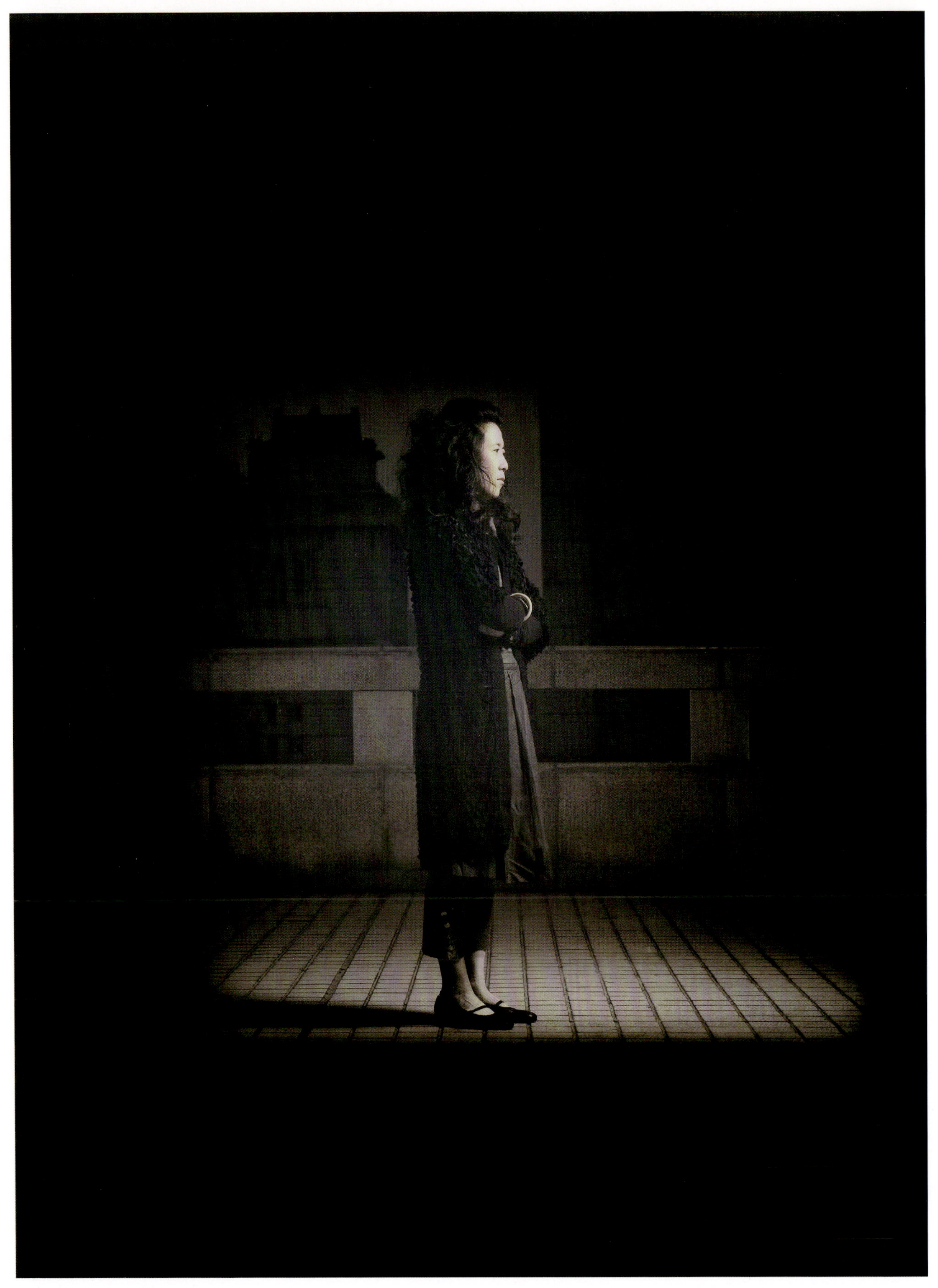

VIRGILE SIMON BERTRAND
YIN XIU ZHEN, ARTIST, BEIJING
APRIL 2008

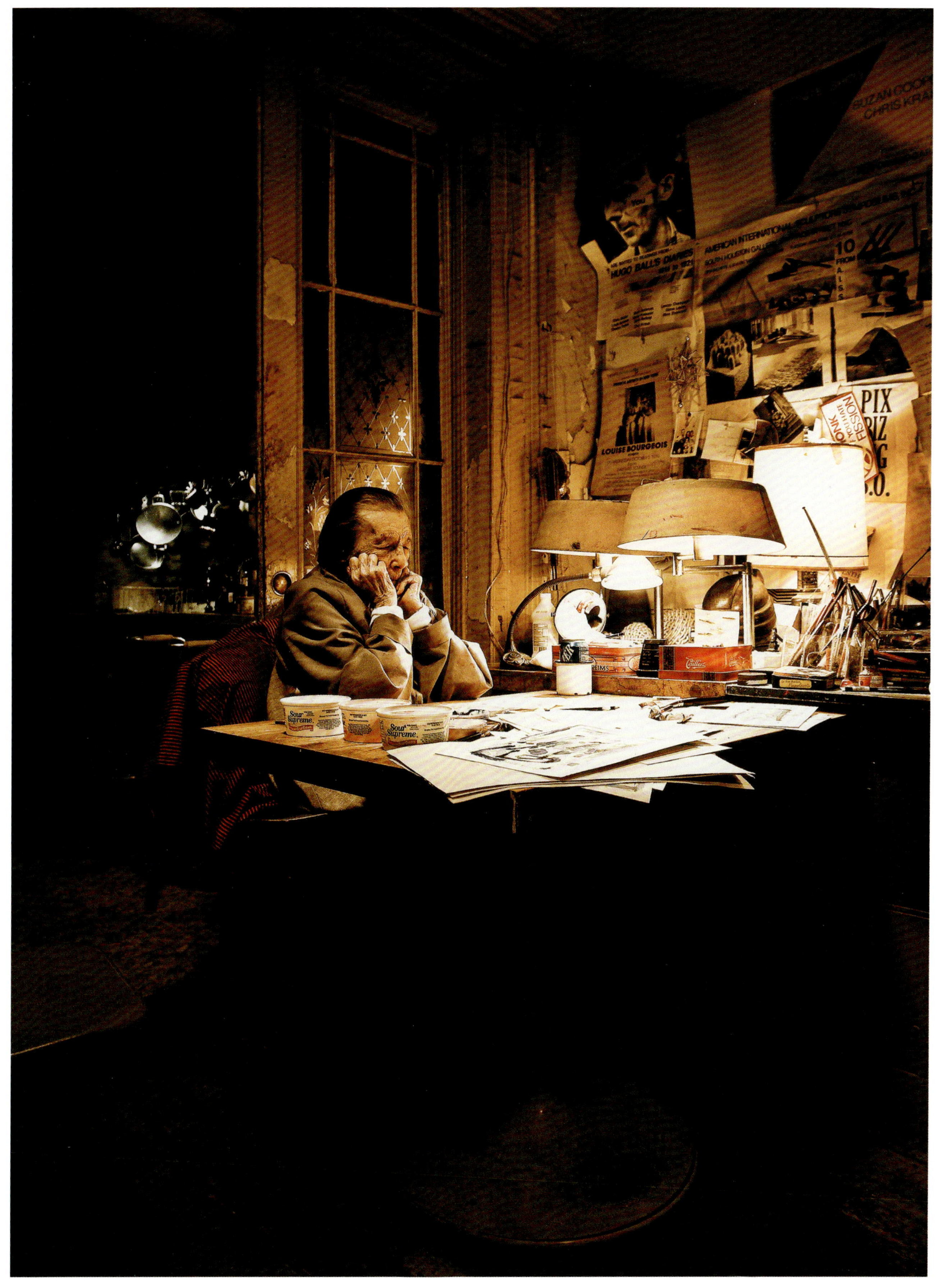

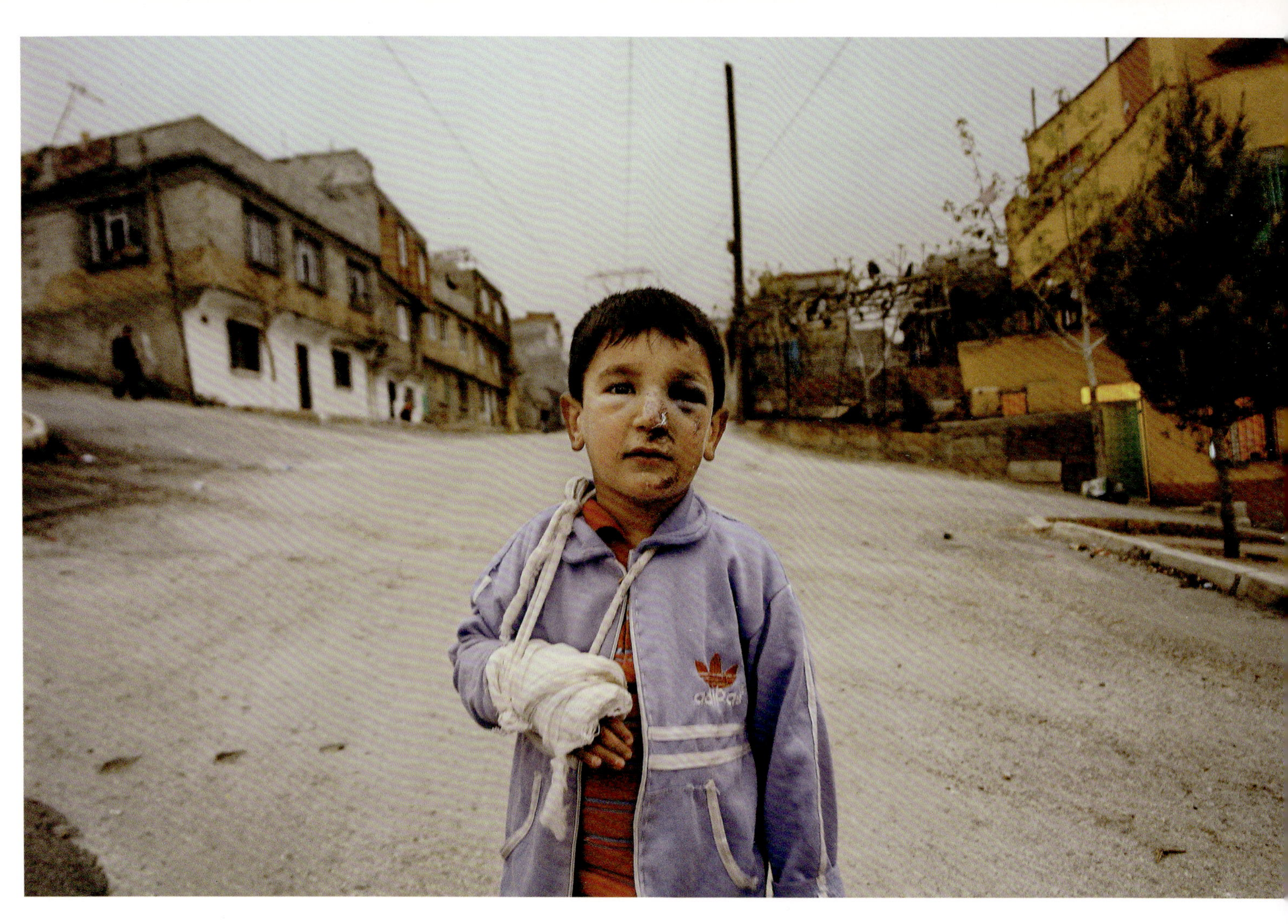

GEORGE GEORGIOU
TURKISH KURD BOY
FROM THE SERIES
HAPPY IS HE WHO CALLS HIMSELF A TURK
MAY 2007

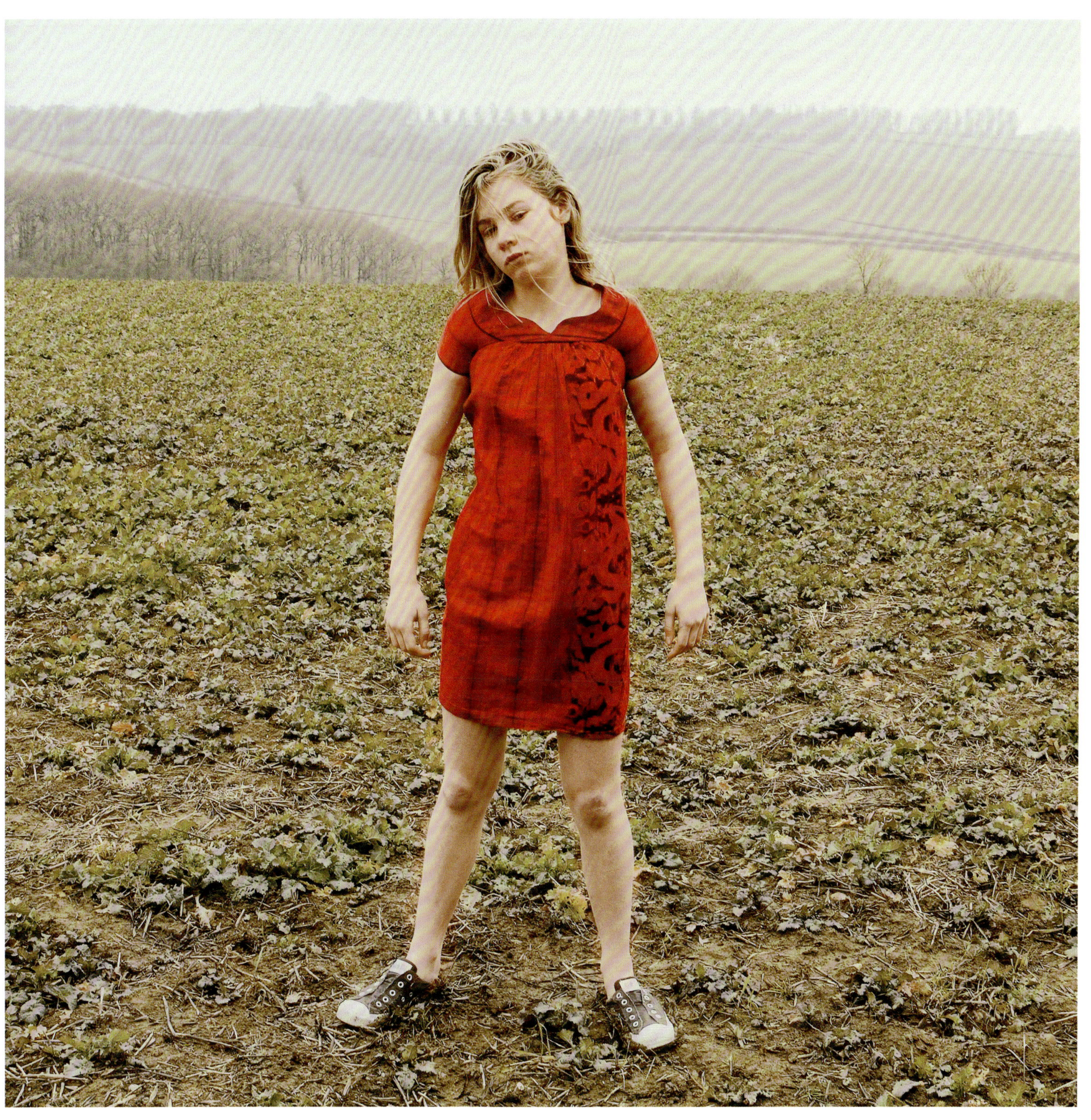

ATALANTA MARCHESSINI
MILLIE
MARCH 2007

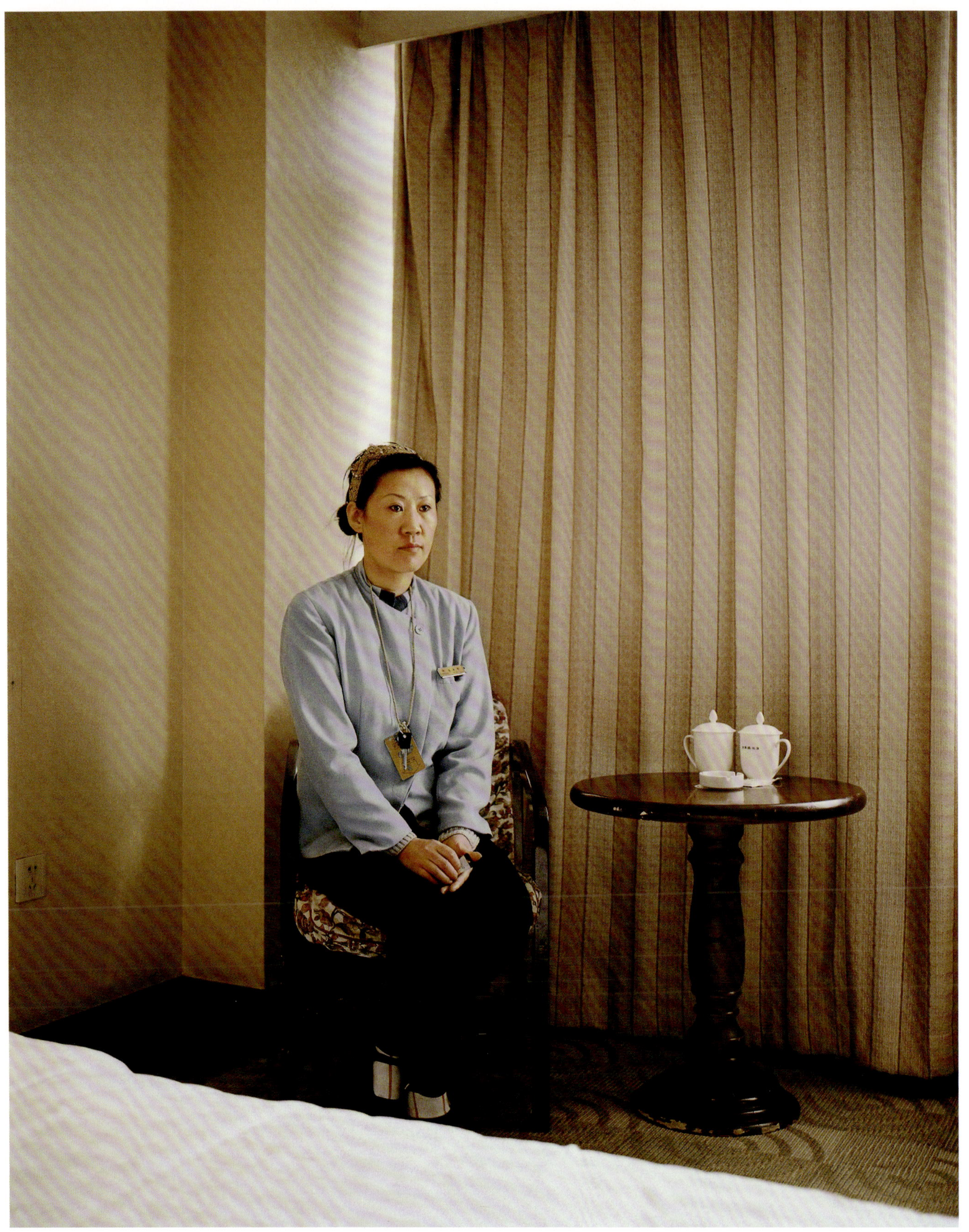

WANG WEI

STANDARD ROOM NO.11
FROM THE SERIES *STANDARD ROOM*
APRIL 2007

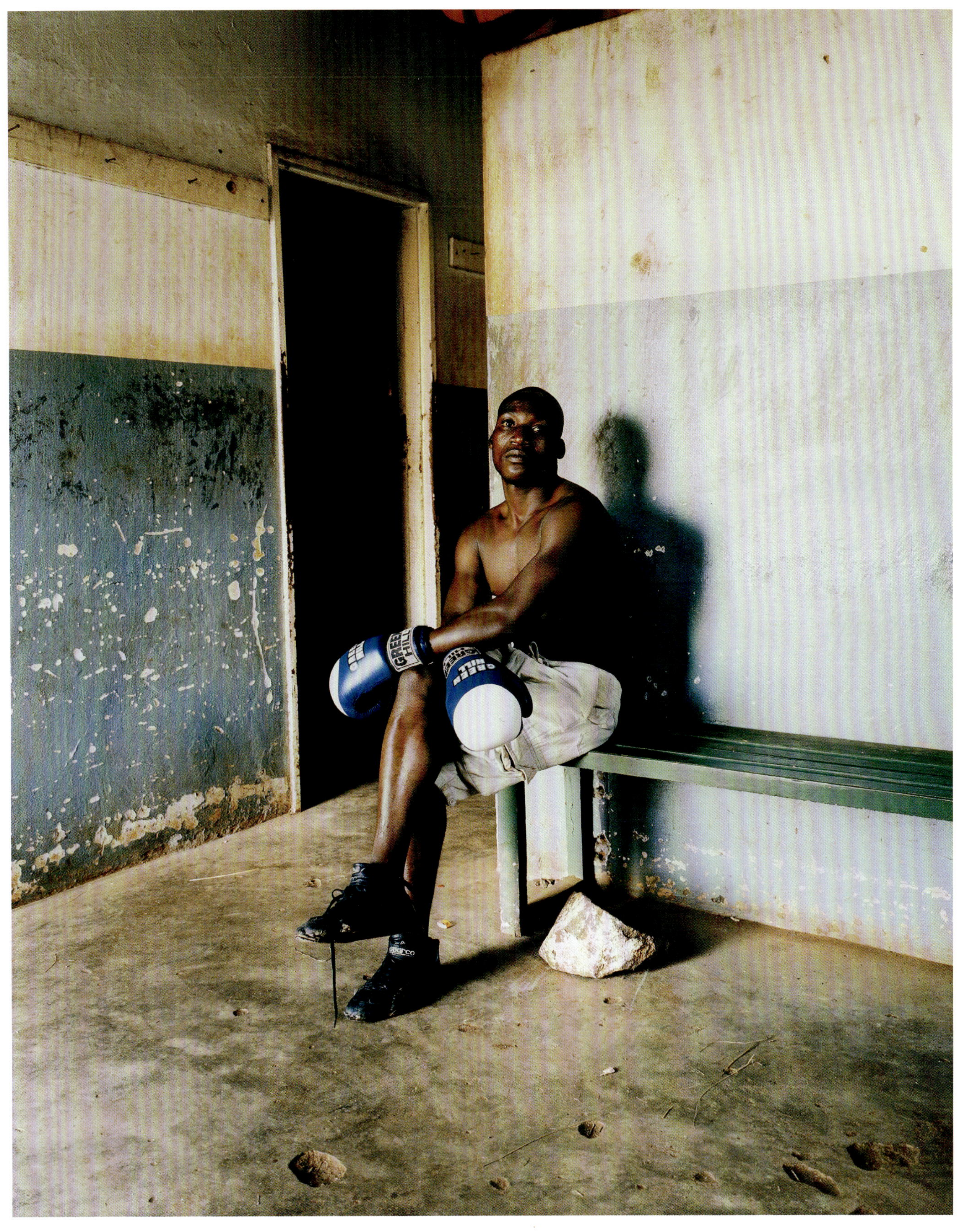

LUCA J. SAGE
WELLINGTON, ZOMBA BOXING CLUB
FROM THE SERIES
NOTES ON RAIN STOPPING IN NYASALAND
APRIL 2007

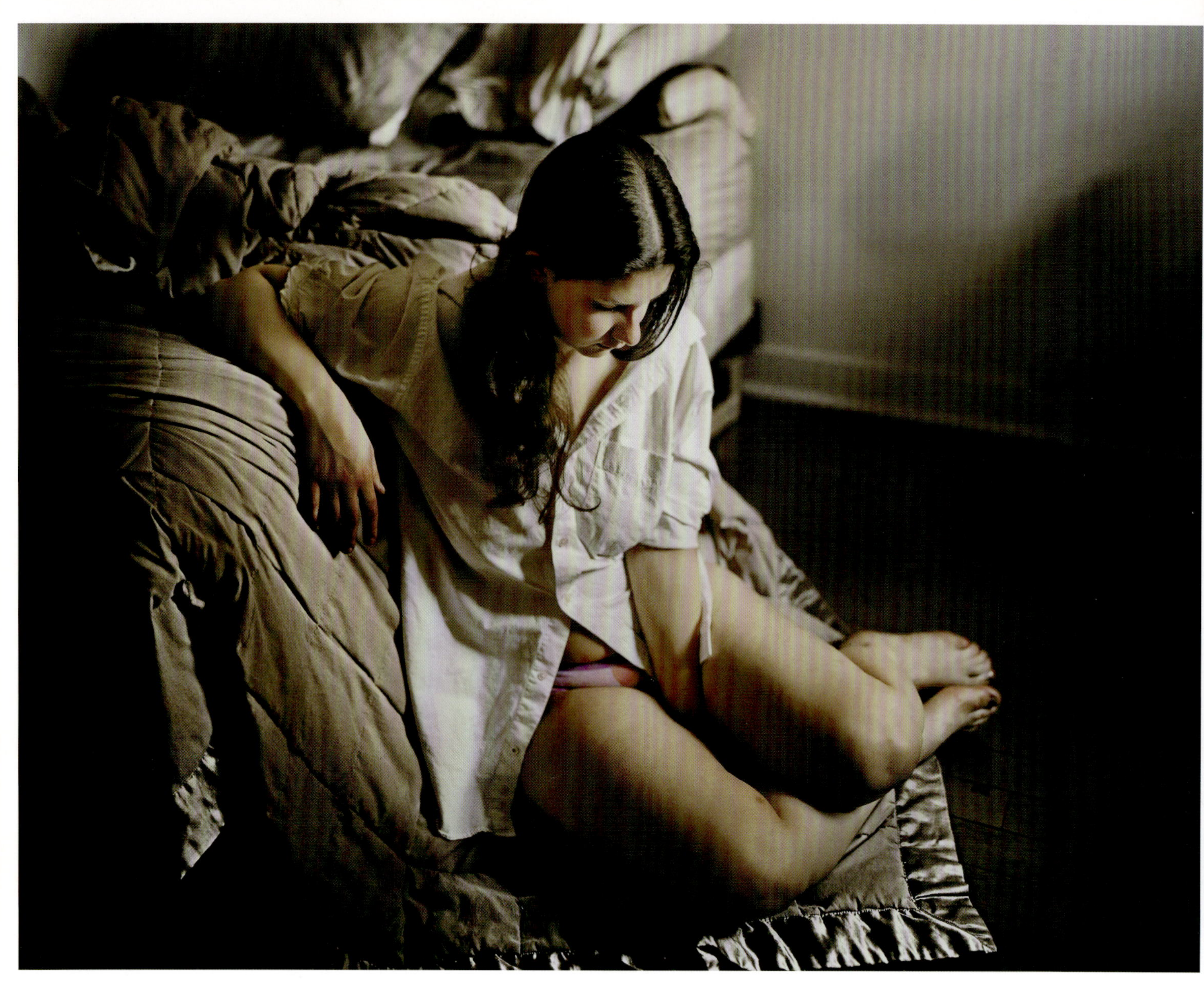

HERMAN NICHOLSON
UNTITLED NO. 6
FROM THE SERIES
STAND GUARD OVER THE SOLITUDE OF THE OTHER
MAY 2008

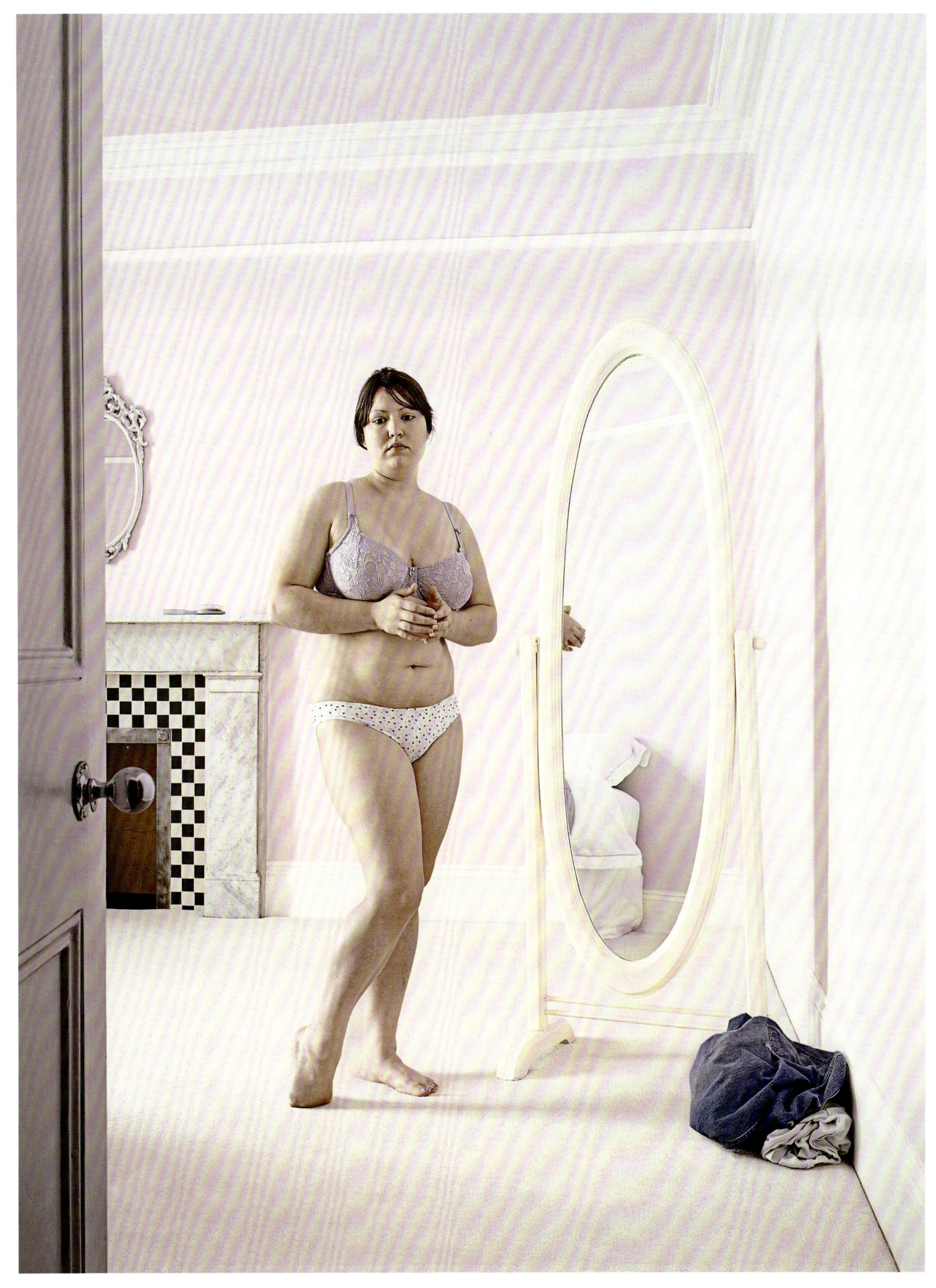

KELVIN MURRAY
GIRL AND MIRROR
MAY 2008

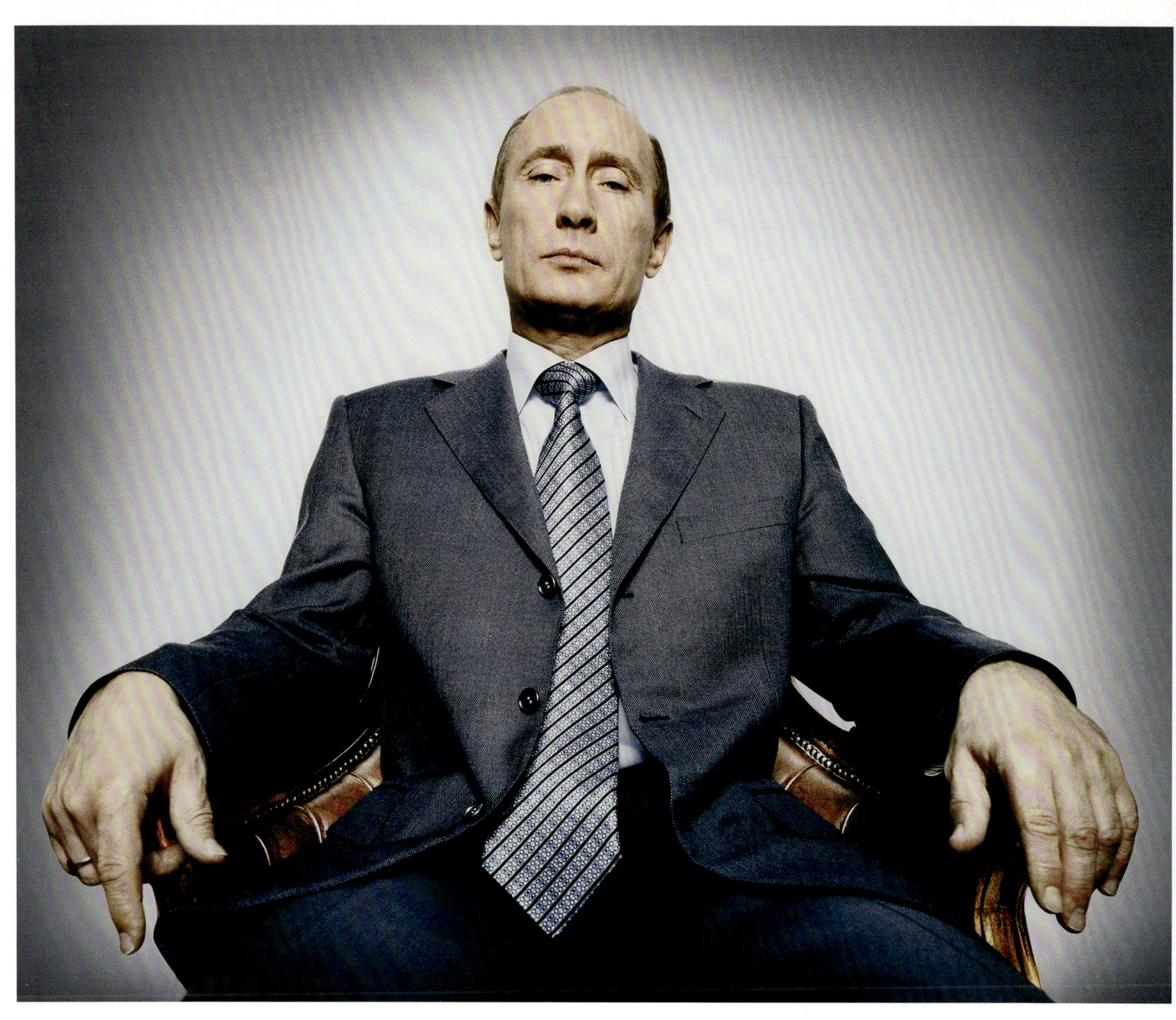

PLATON ANTONIOU
VLADIMIR VLADIMIROVICH PUTIN
DECEMBER 2007

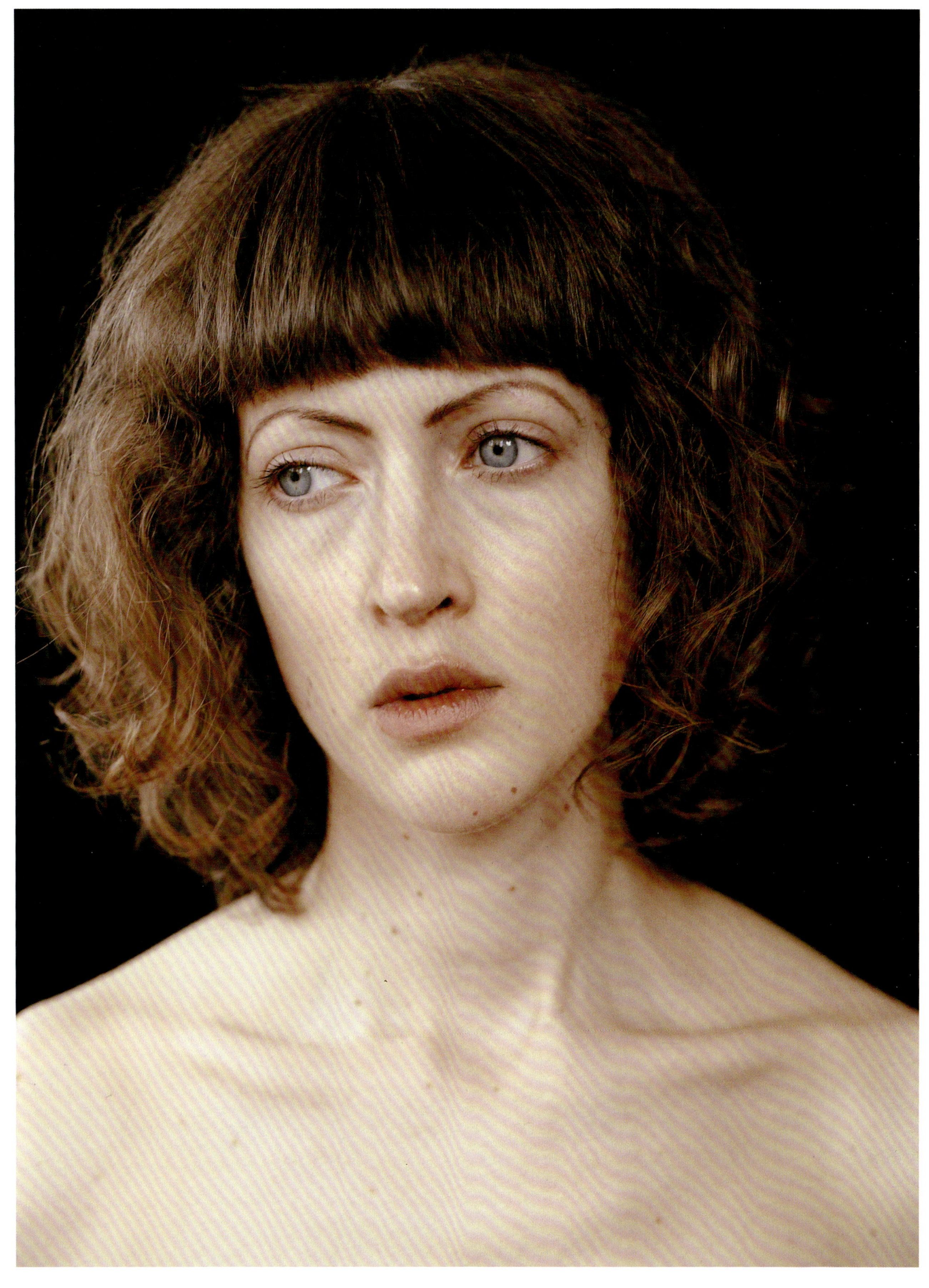

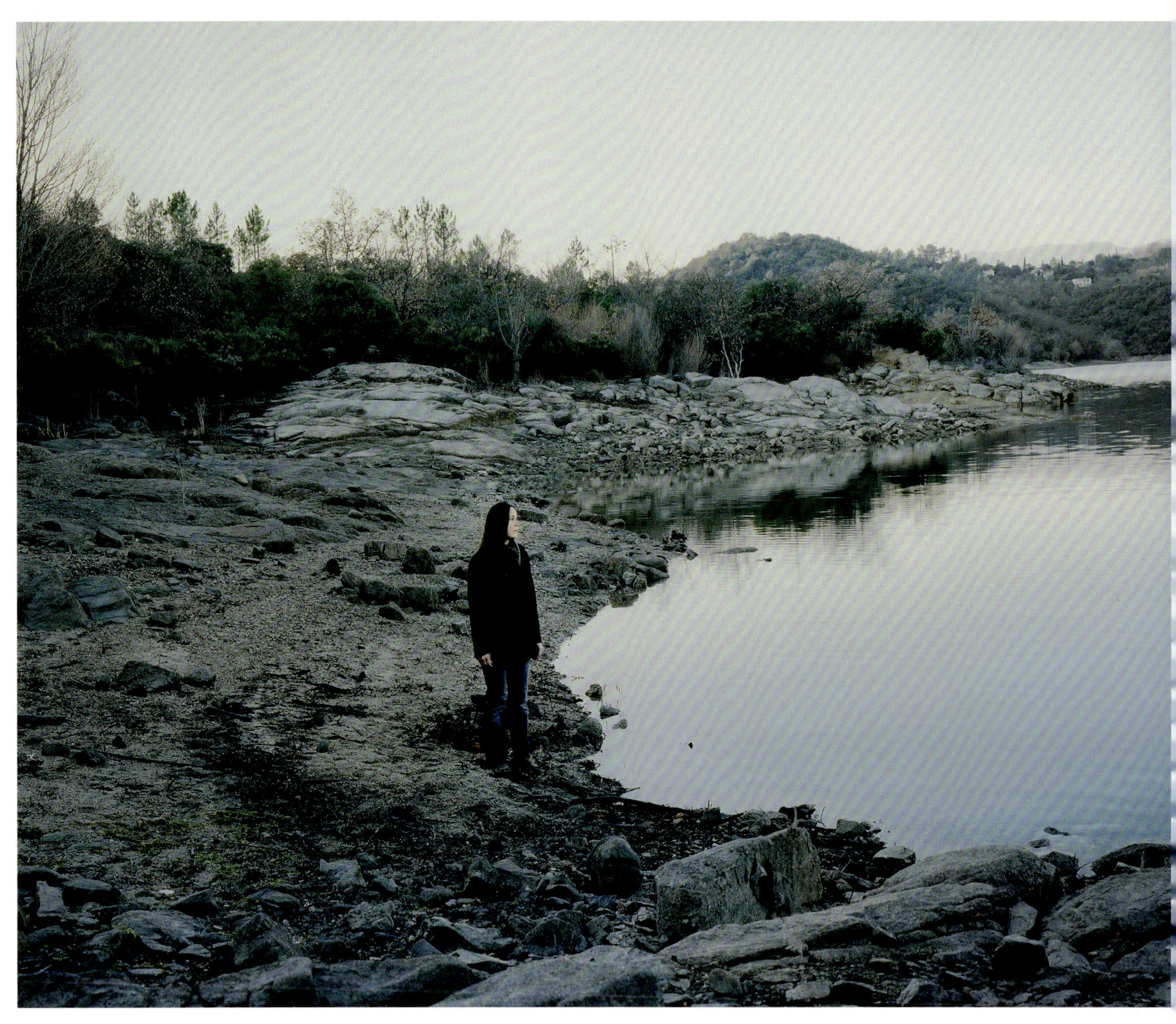

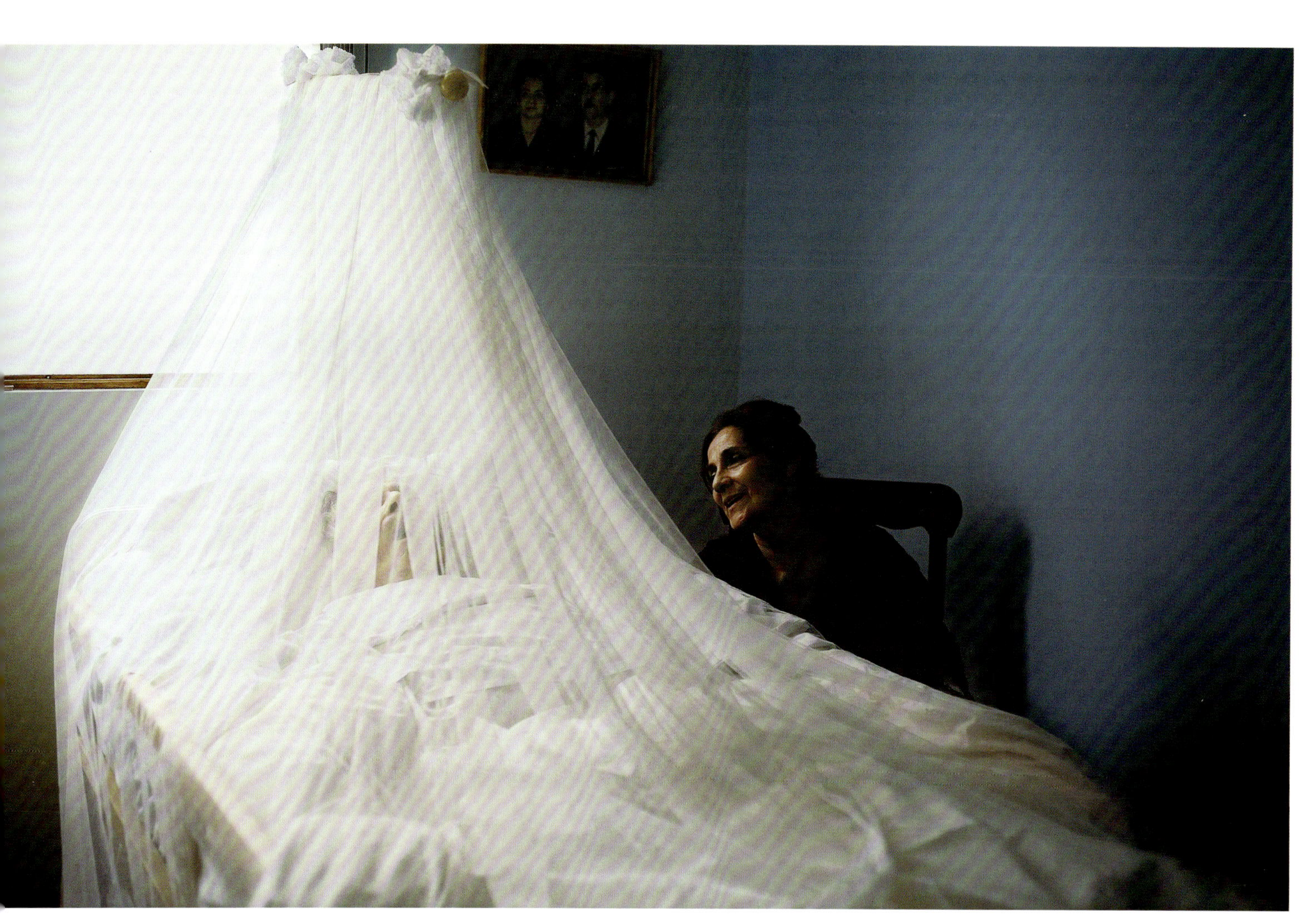

PALOMA PARGAC
100 YEARS OF LOVE
FROM THE SERIES
MI FAMILIA PERUANA (MY PERUVIAN FAMILY)
JANUARY 2007

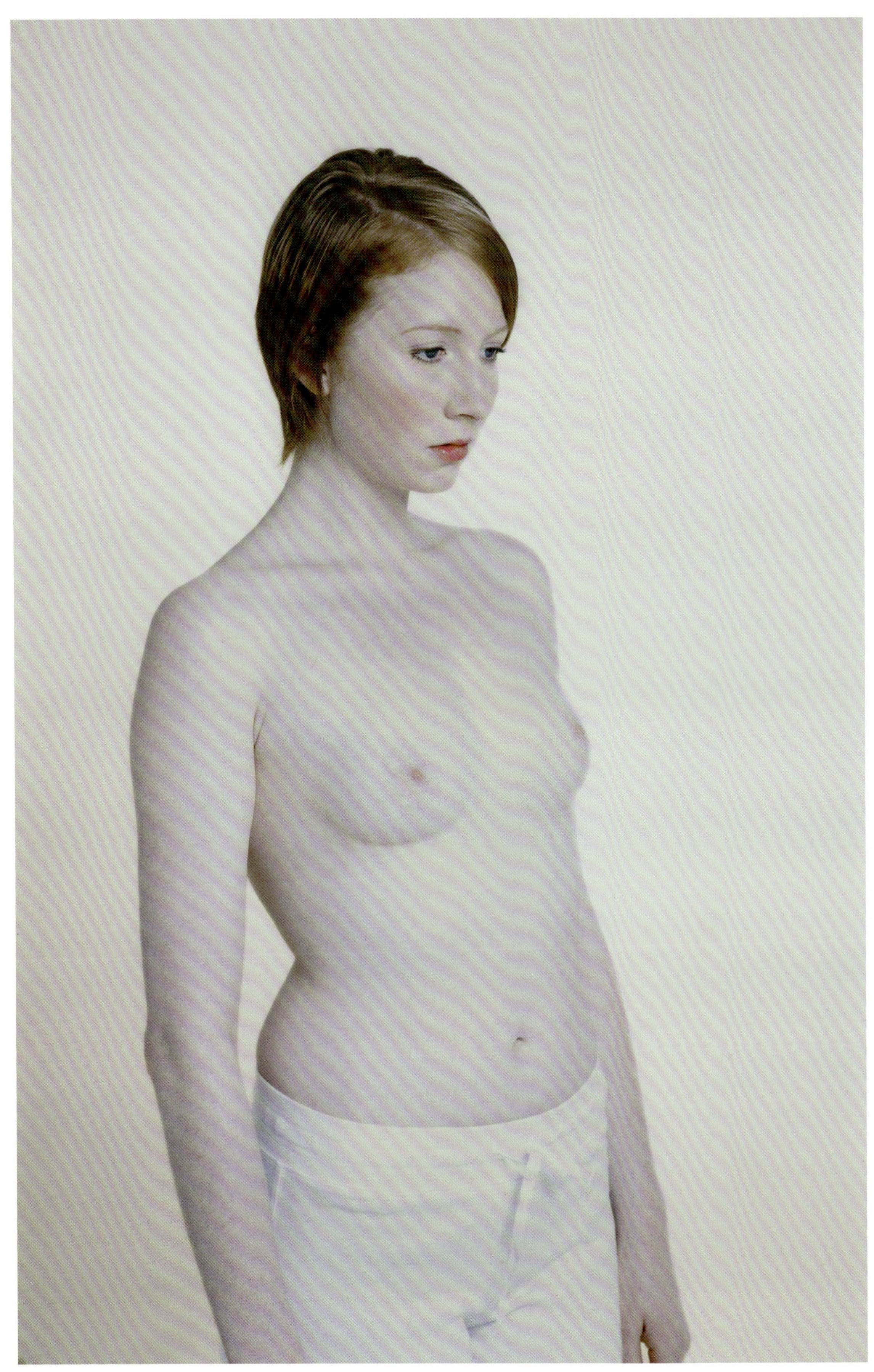

JONATHAN FORD
ROSIE
APRIL 2008

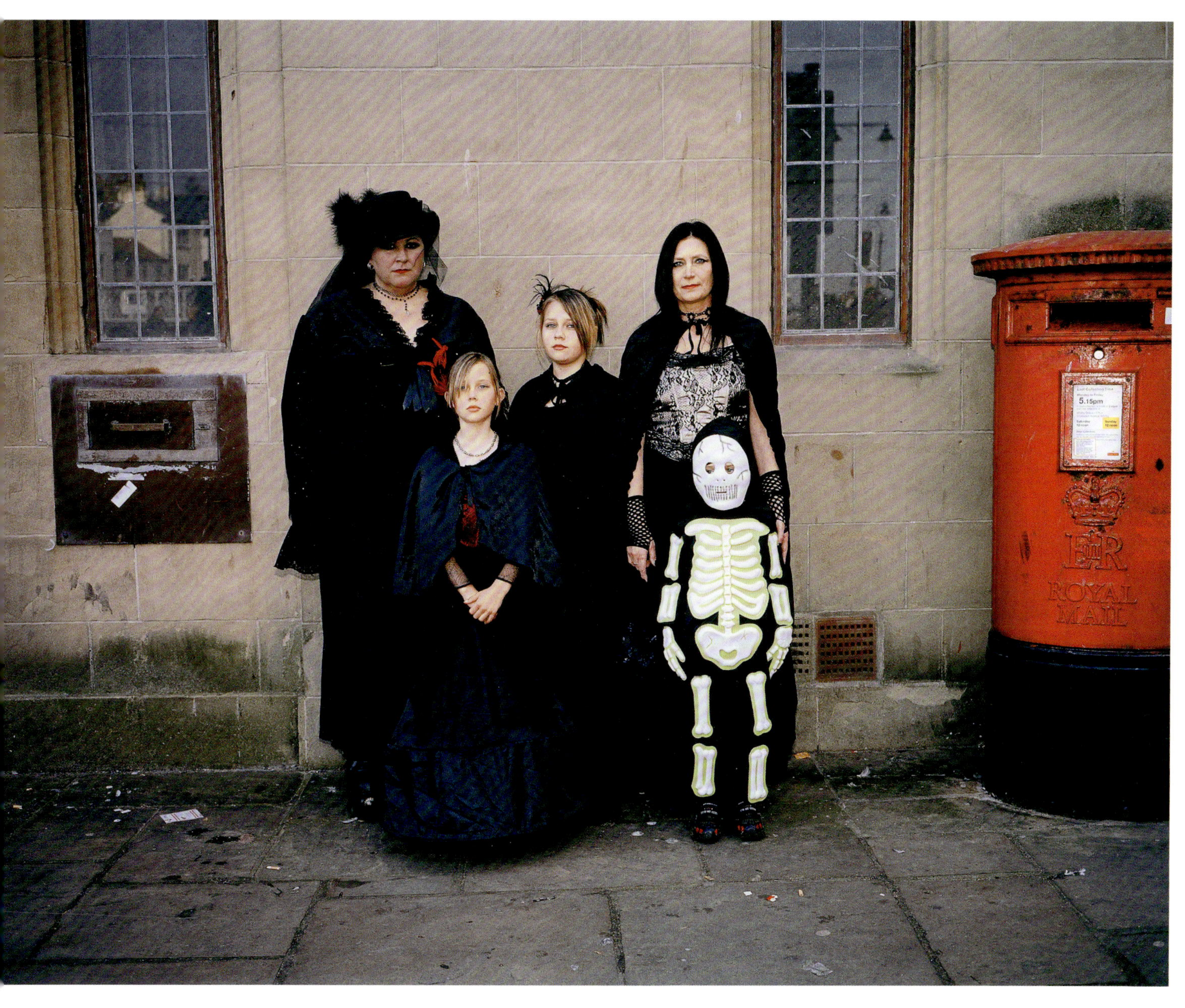

DUNCAN MCKENZIE
WHITBY
FROM THE SERIES
WHITBY GOTHIC WEEKEND FESTIVAL
OCTOBER 2007

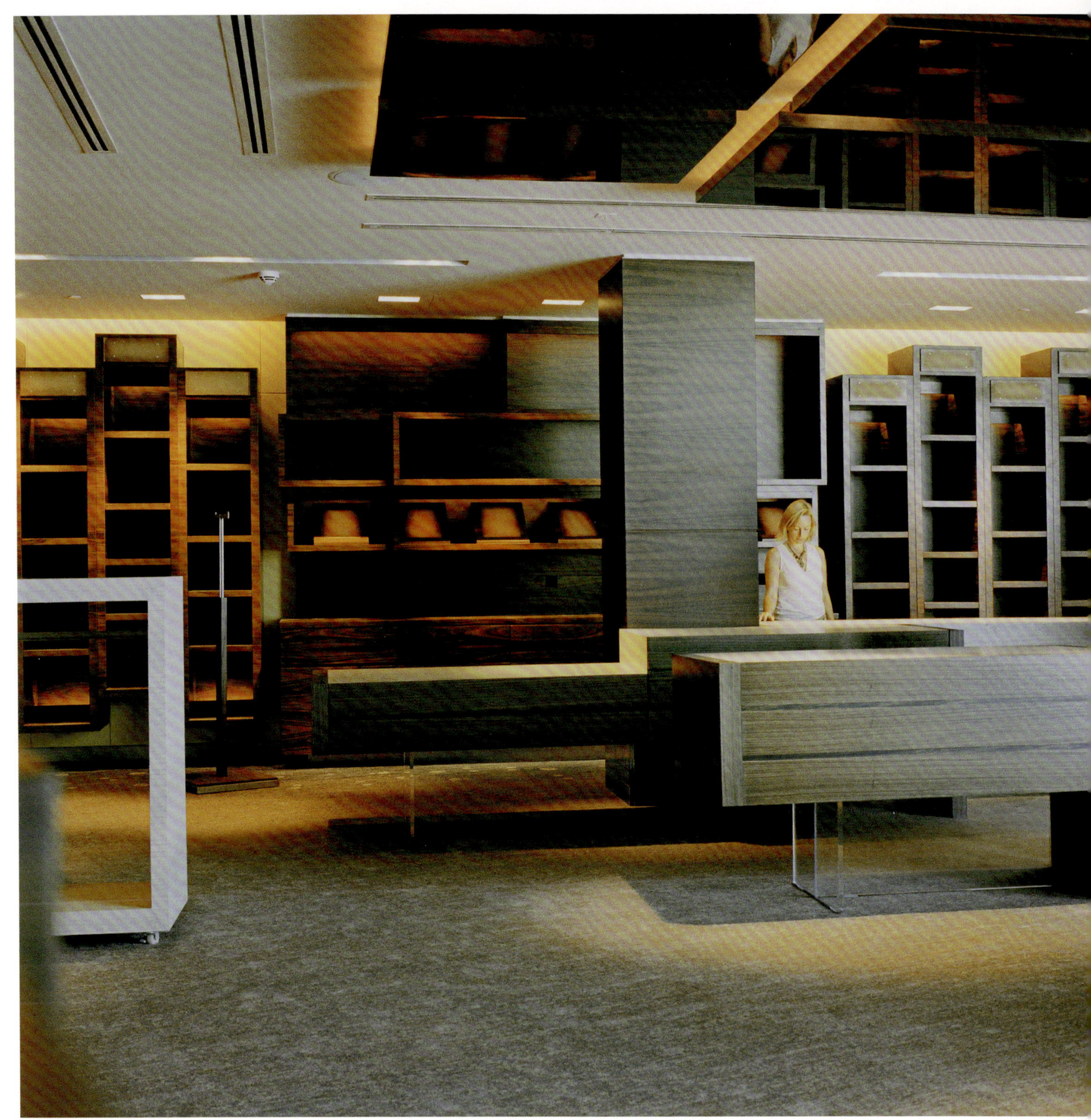

SUE PARKHILL

SHOP
FROM THE SERIES
COMMITTED CONSUMERS
NOVEMBER 2007

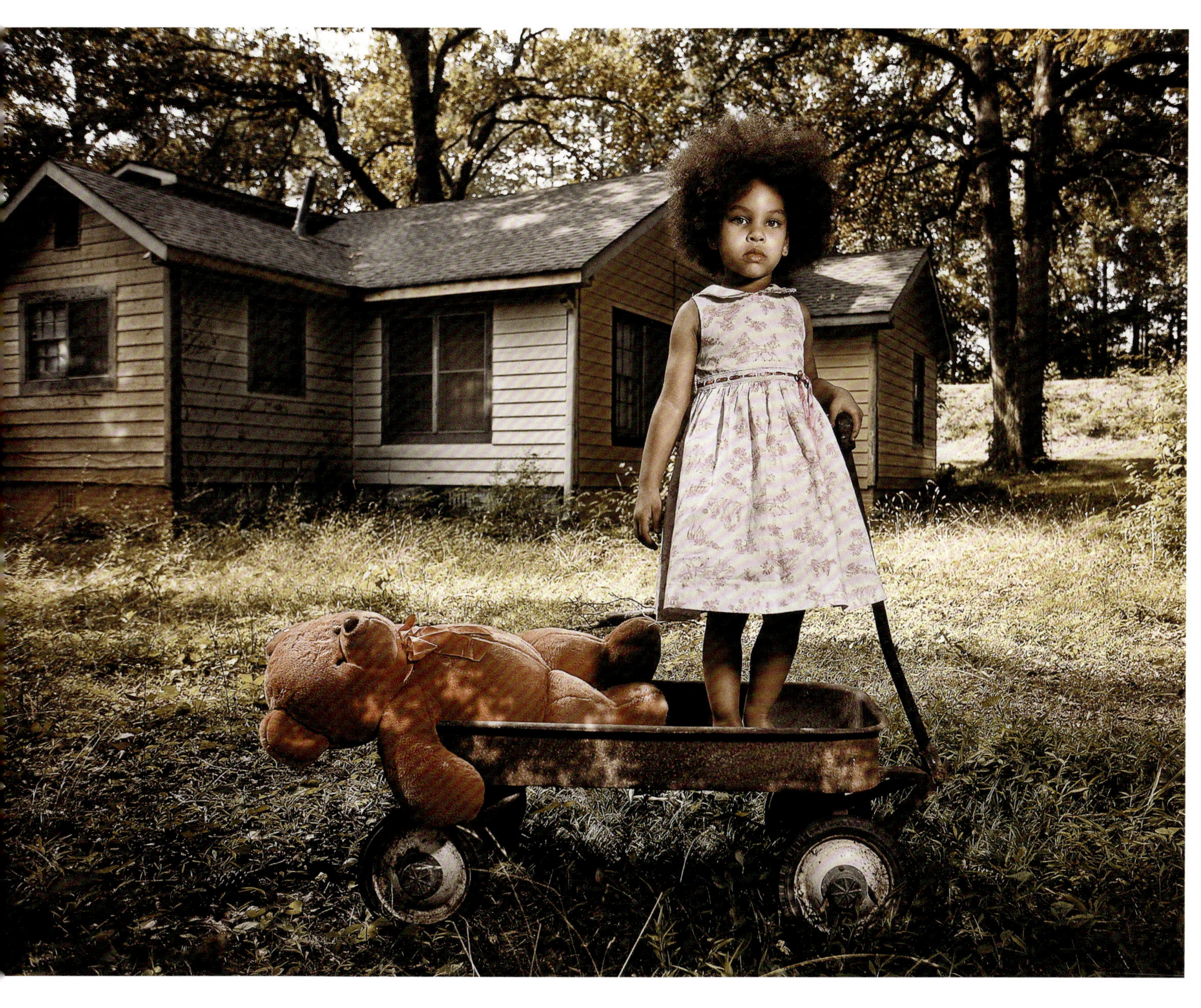

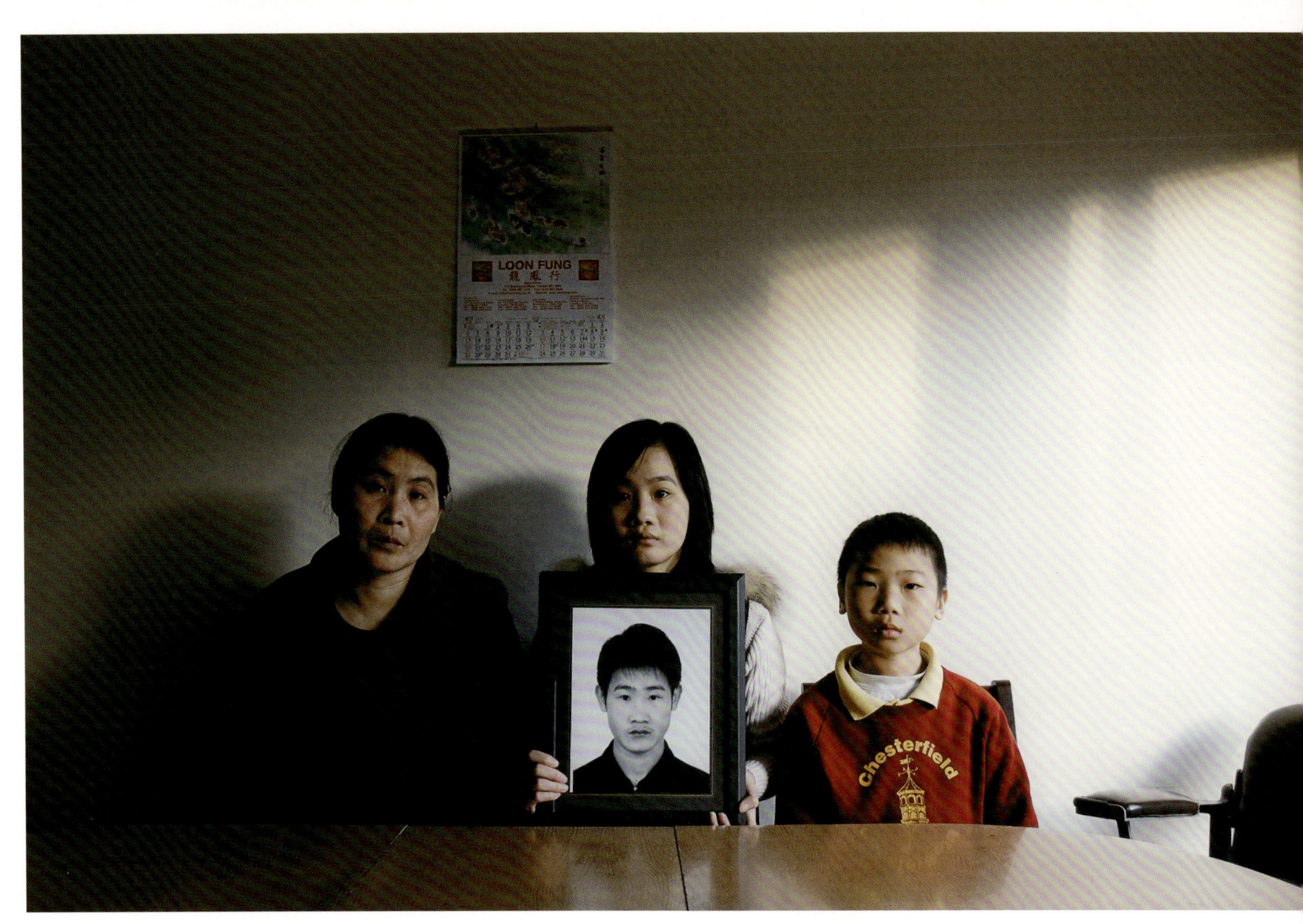

TOBY NG

UNCOVERED
FROM THE SERIES *LI TAN*
FEBRUARY 2008

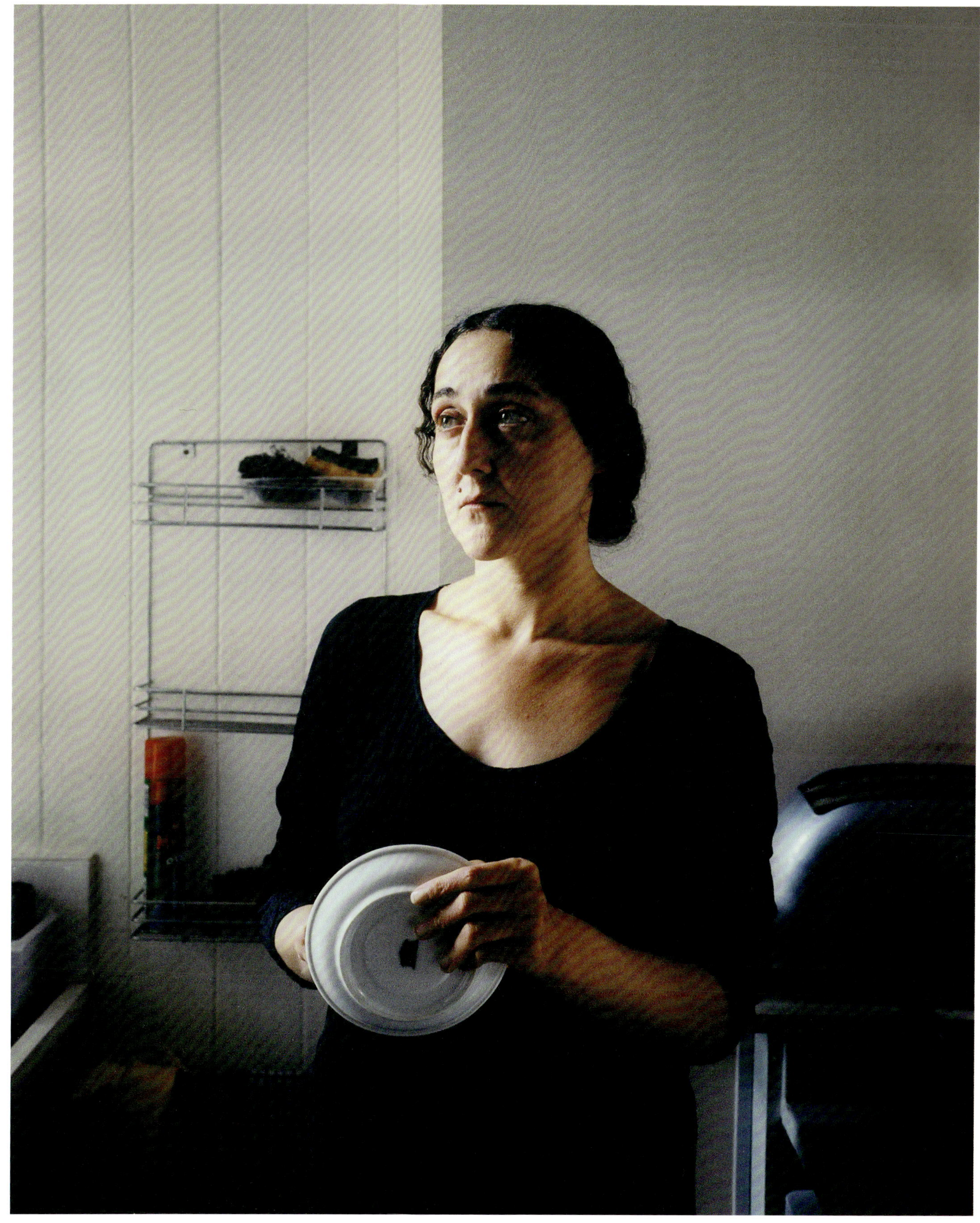

BESO UZNADZE
TINA
FROM THE SERIES TBILISI PORTRAITS
OCTOBER 2007

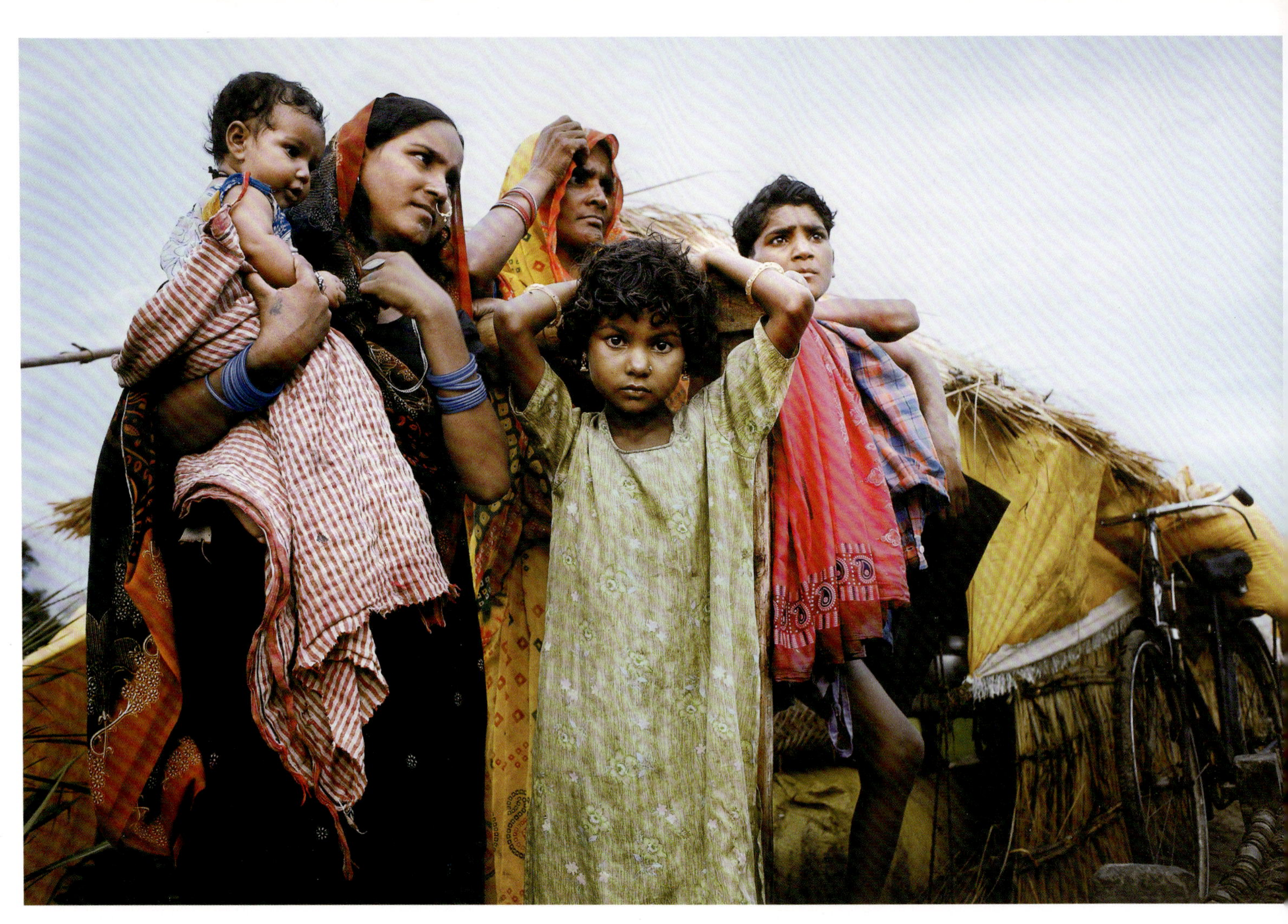

TOM PIETRASIK

SANGITA AND HER FAMILY
FROM THE SERIES
FLOOD-AFFECTED COMMUNITIES ACROSS NORTH INDIA
AUGUST 2007

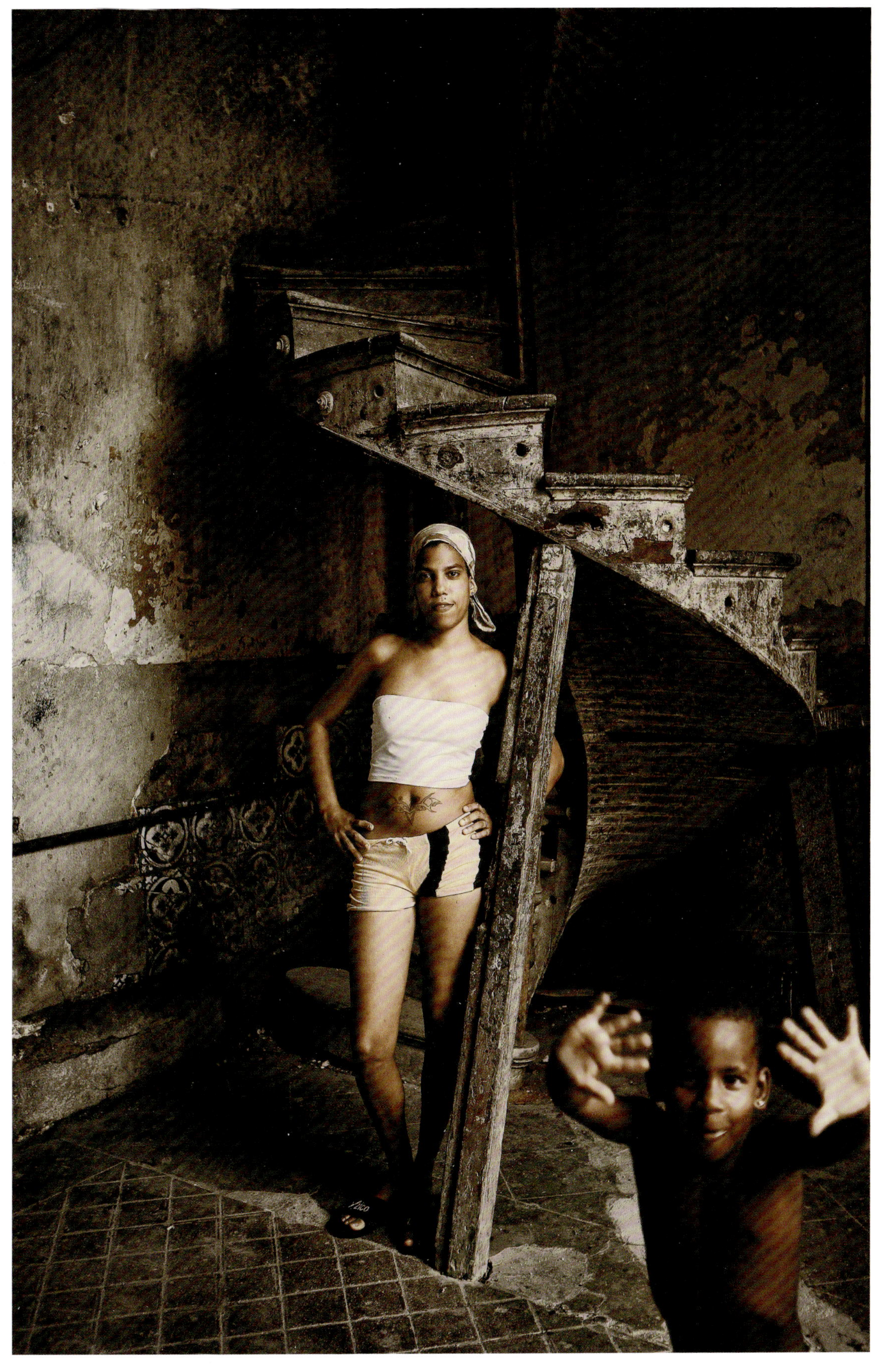

GEORGE FETTING
CHICA AND SPIRAL STAIRCASE, HAVANA
FROM THE SERIES *CUBA'S OLD CITY*
SEPTEMBER 2007

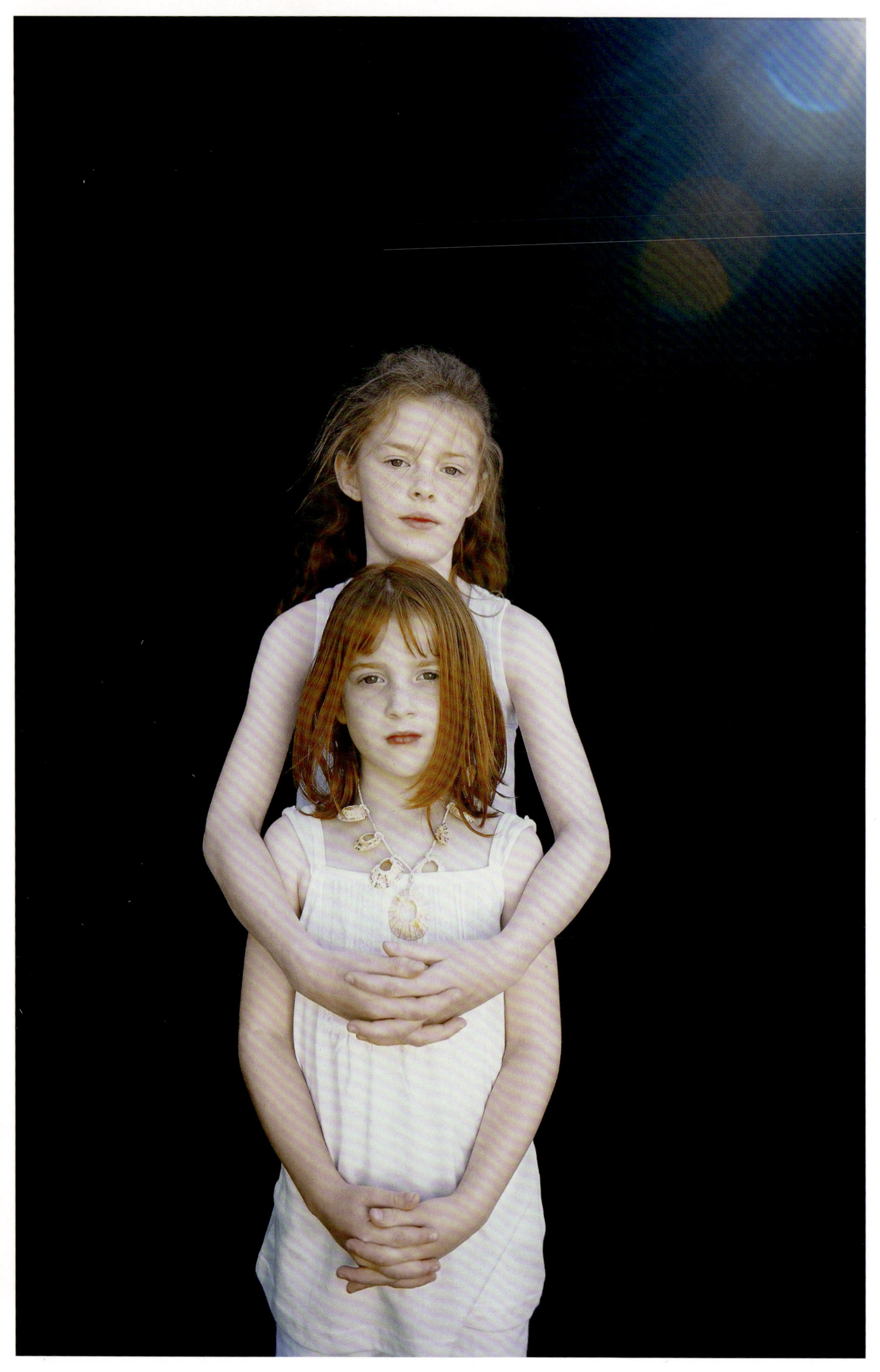

JANIE AIREY
HANNAH AND JEN IN CORNWALL
JUNE 2008

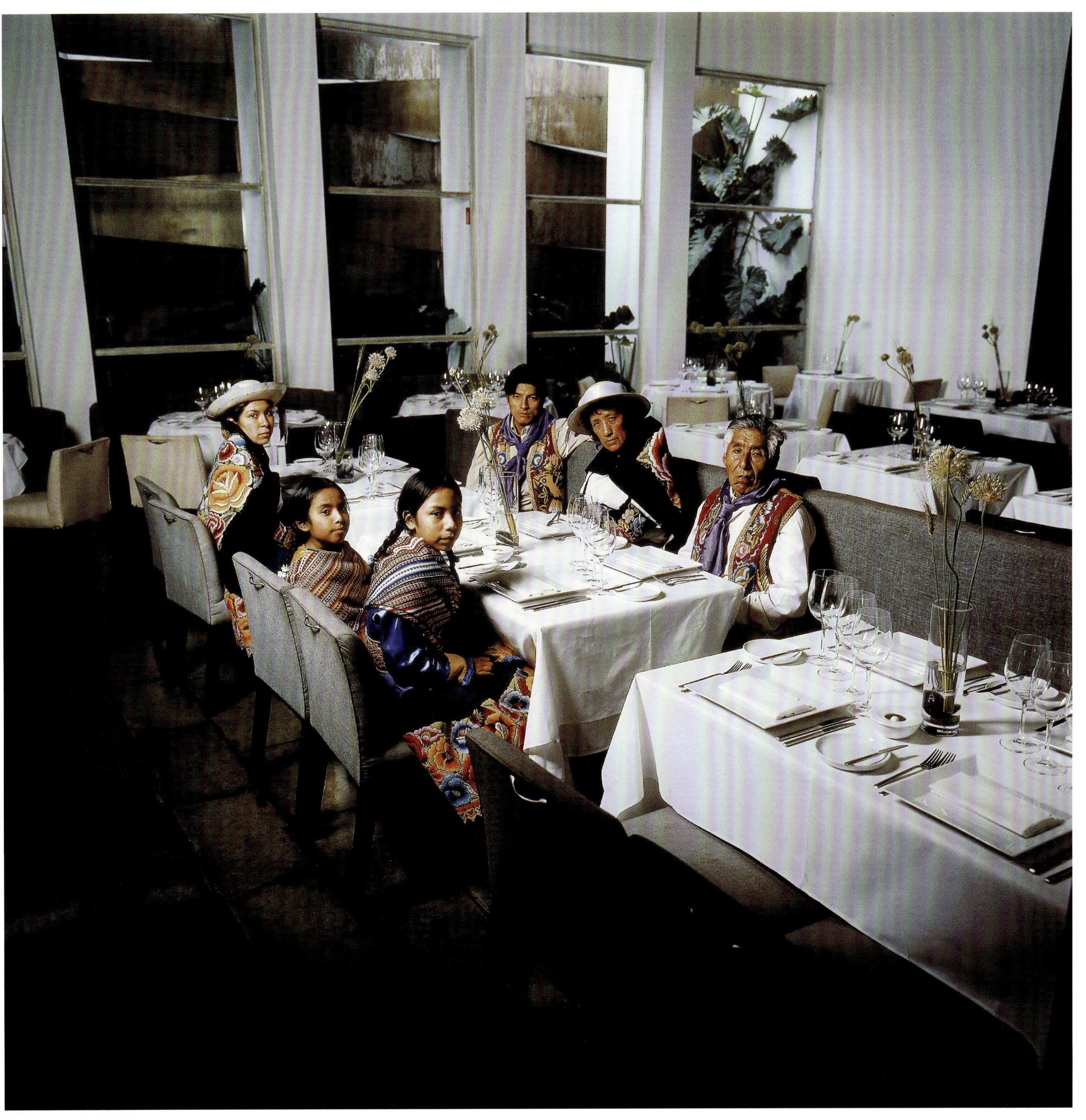

COLECTIVO MR
MARINA GARCÍA BURGOS
AND RICARDO RAMÓN
RESTAURANT
FROM THE SERIES
IF THERE IS NO AFTERLIFE, THE INJUSTICE OF
THE POOR IS PROLONGED ETERNALLY
MARCH 2007

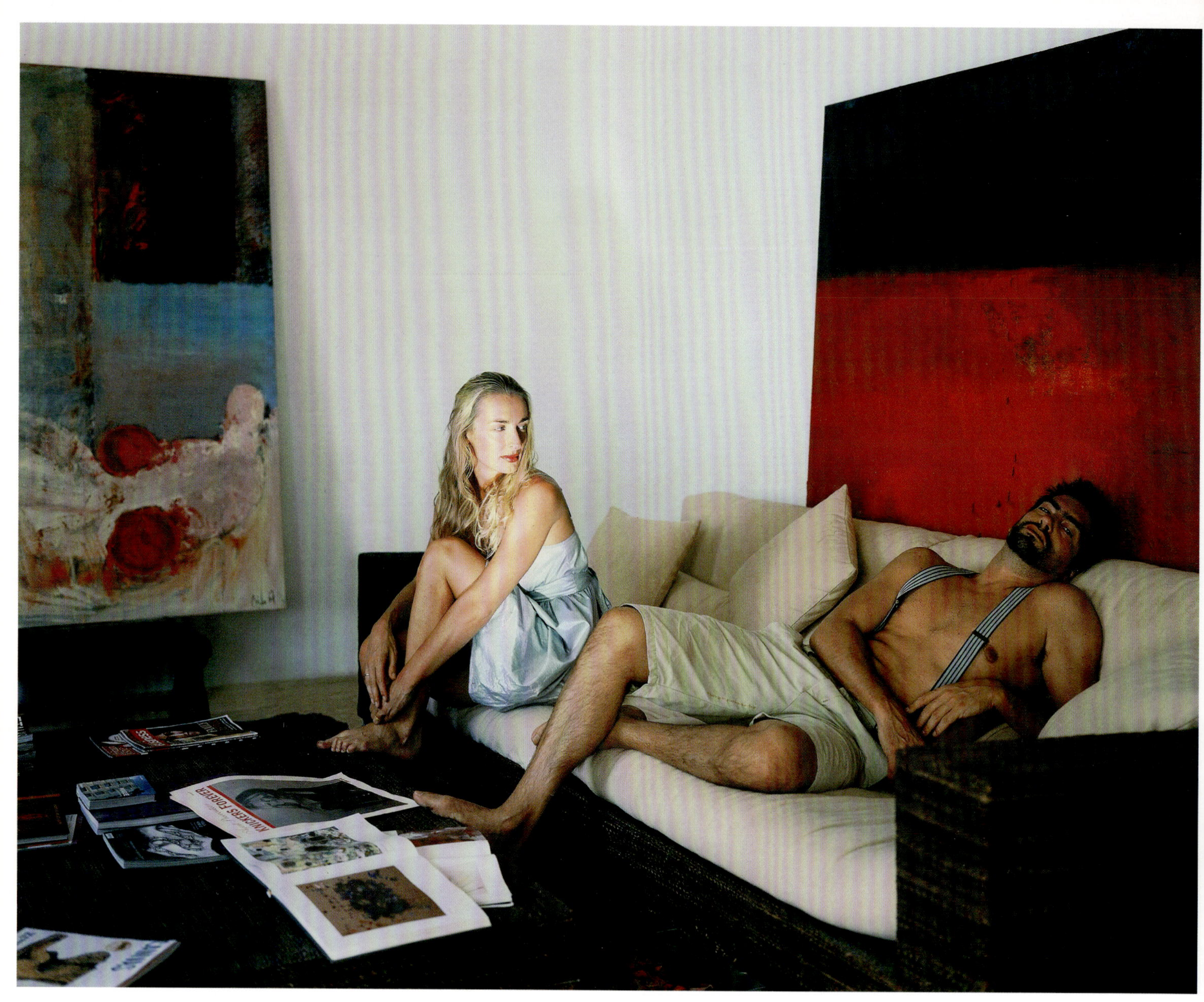

PEDRO ALVAREZ
VERU AND RICARDO
FROM THE SERIES
DUBAI, THEN AND THERE
MARCH 2008

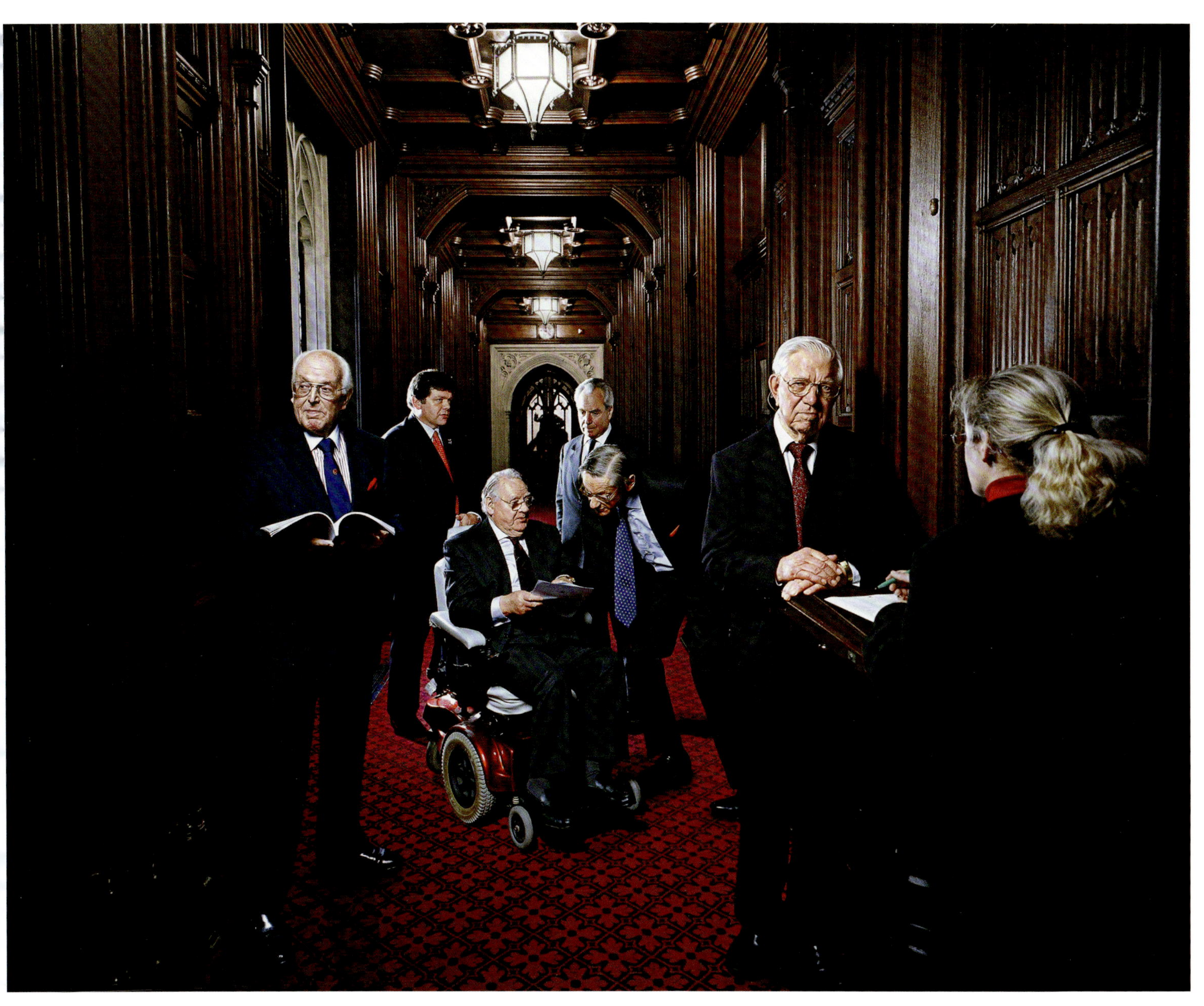

DESIREE PFEIFFER

SPEAKERS ON LORD ASHLEY OF STOKE'S
QUESTION IN THE CONTENT LOBBY
NOVEMBER 2007

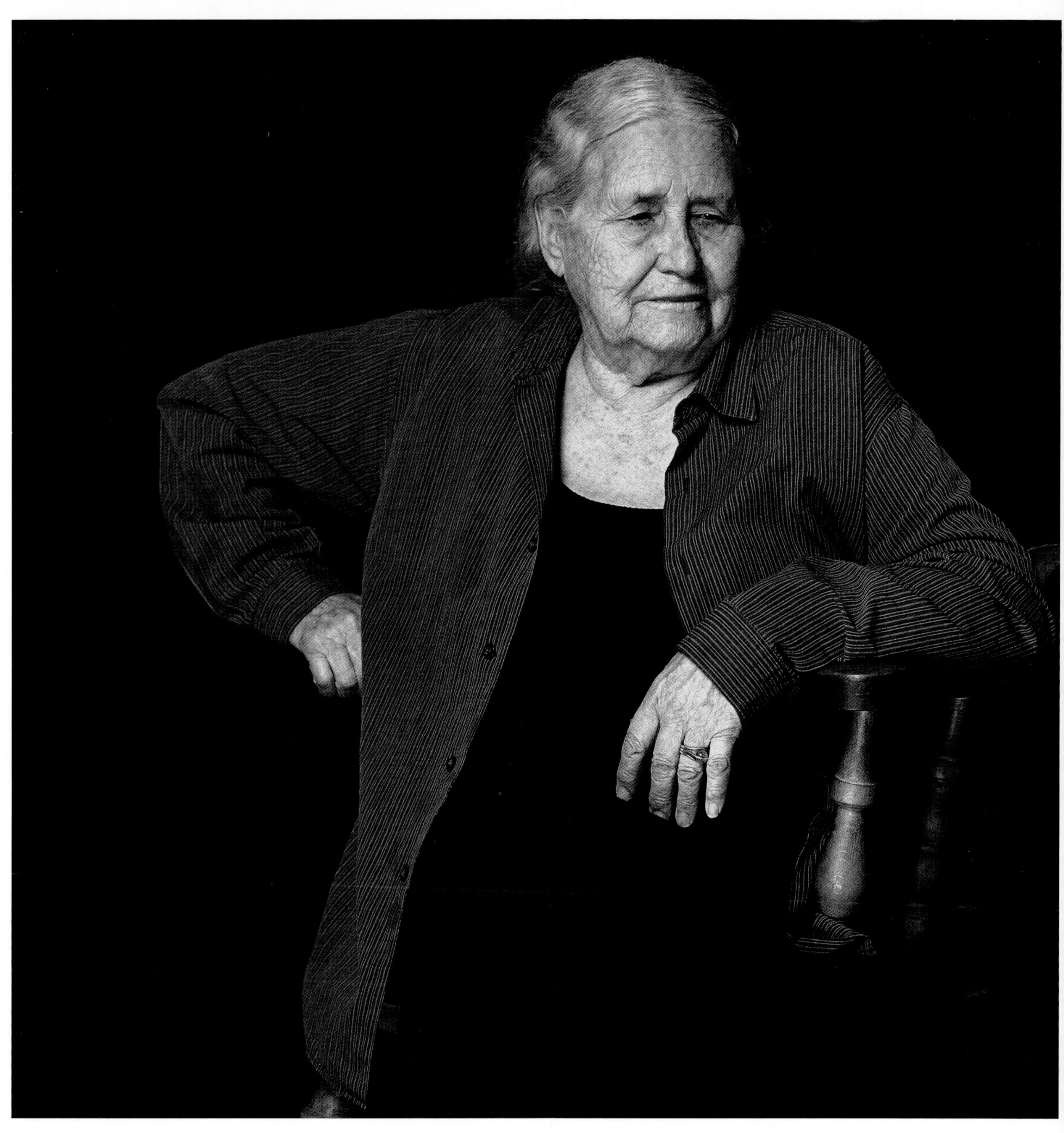

MICHAEL BIRT
DORIS LESSING
JULY 2008

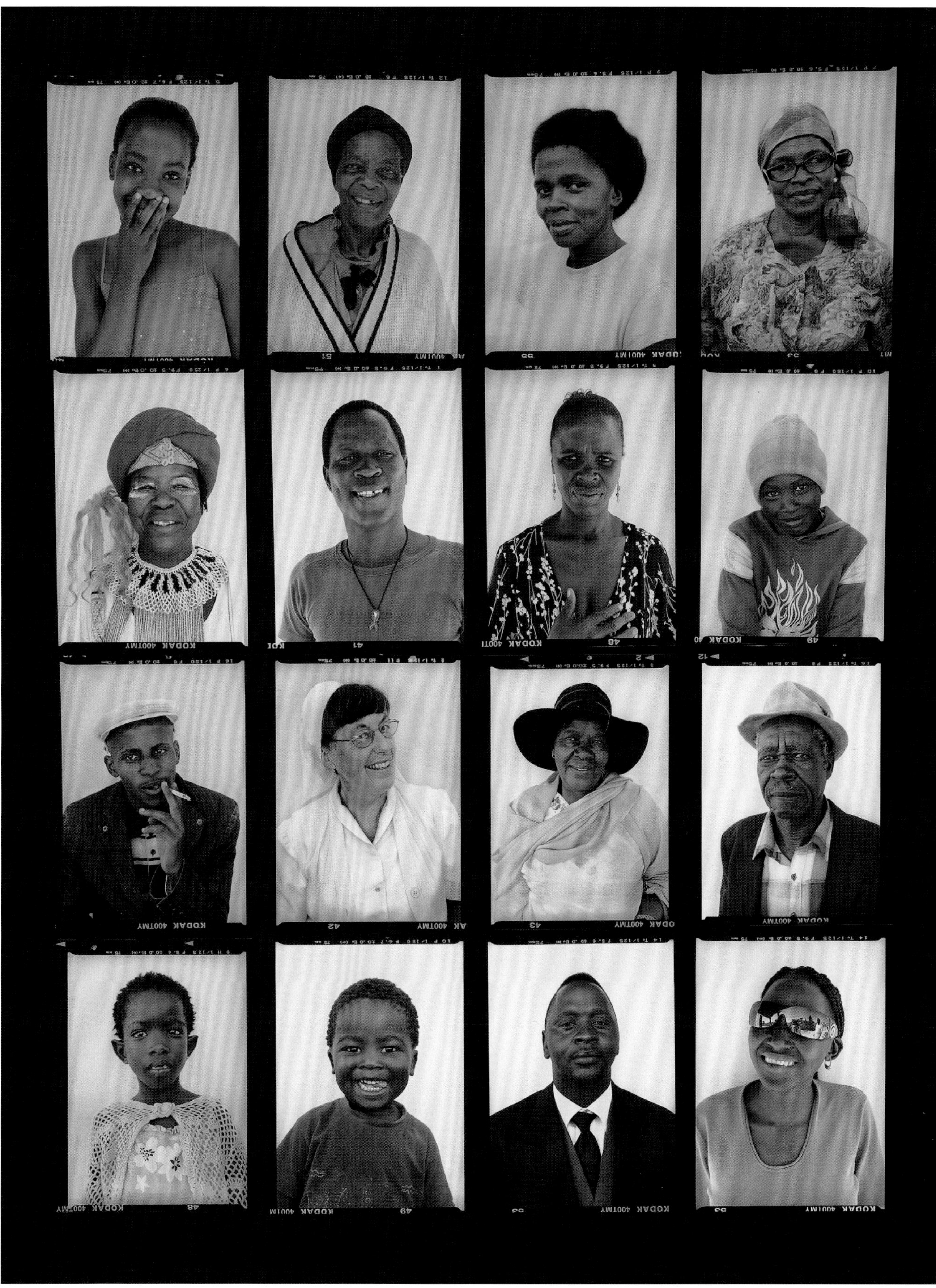

SILVIA AMODIO
POSITIVE FACES
MARCH 2007

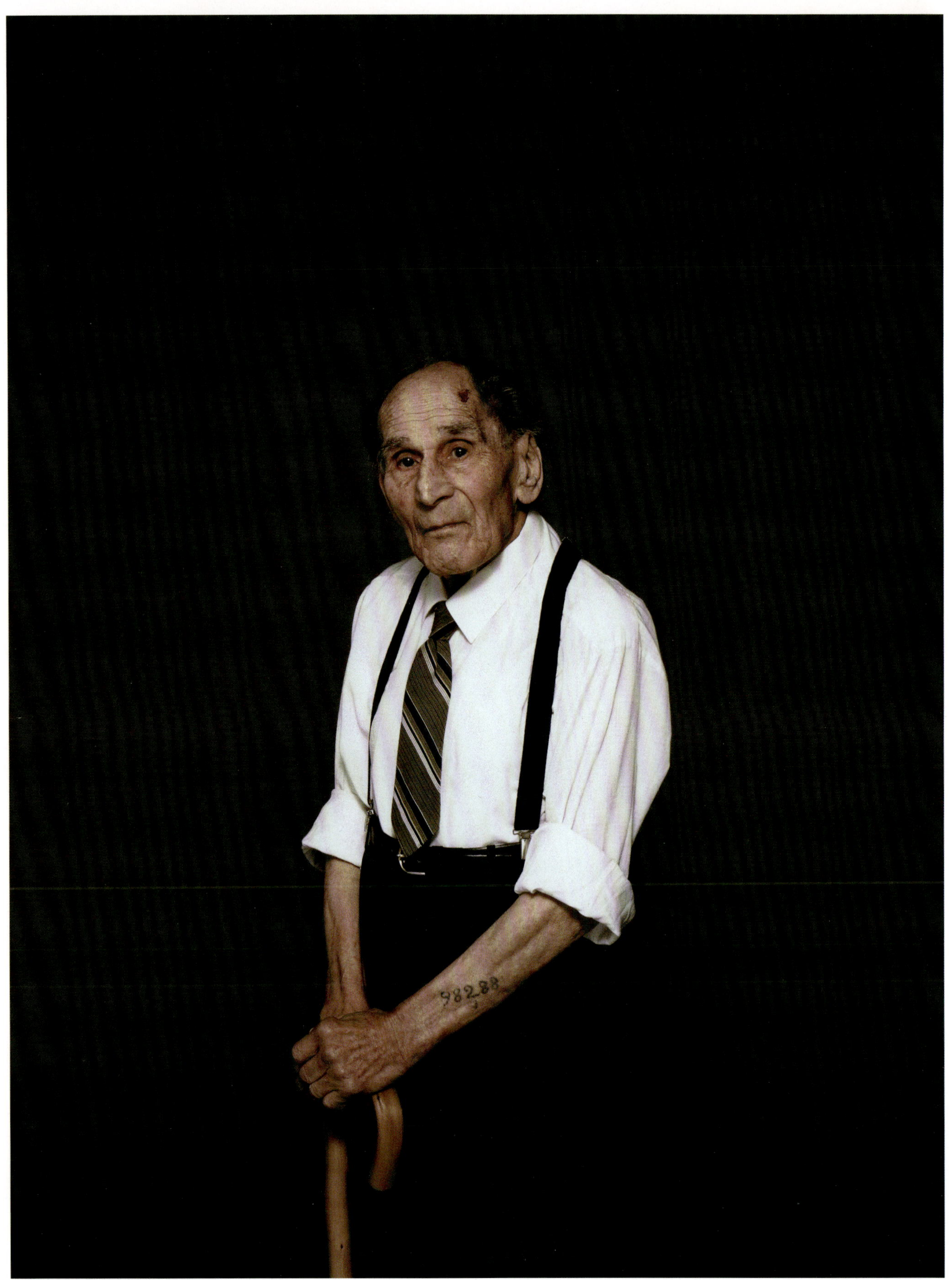

JOEL REDMAN
LEON GREENMAN
DECEMBER 2007

64

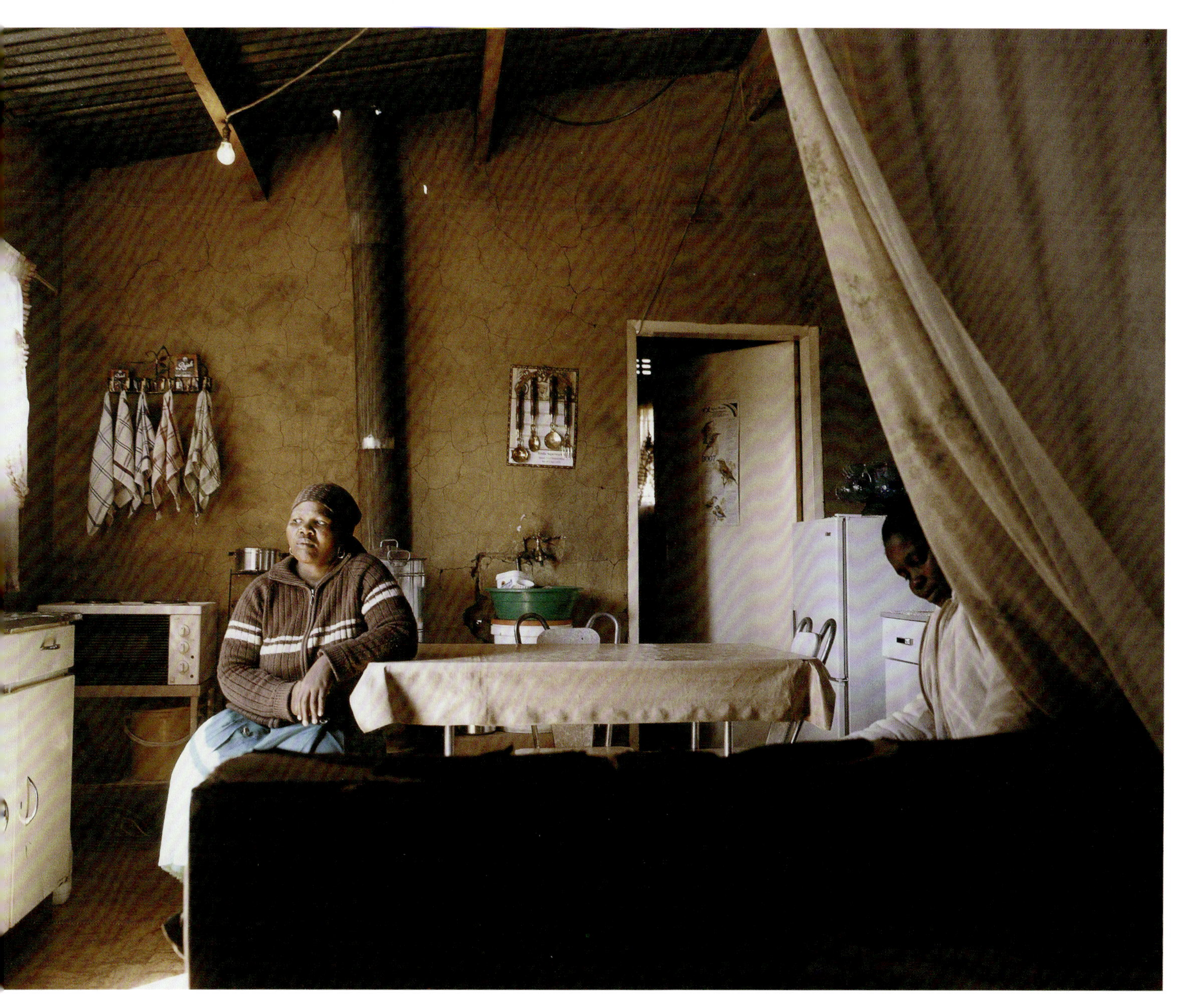

ILAN GODFREY
MARGARET MAHLANGU AND SISTER SELINA,
DUDUZA TOWNSHIP, HYDELBURG
FROM THE SERIES
LIVING WITH CRIME IN SOUTH AFRICA
JUNE 2007

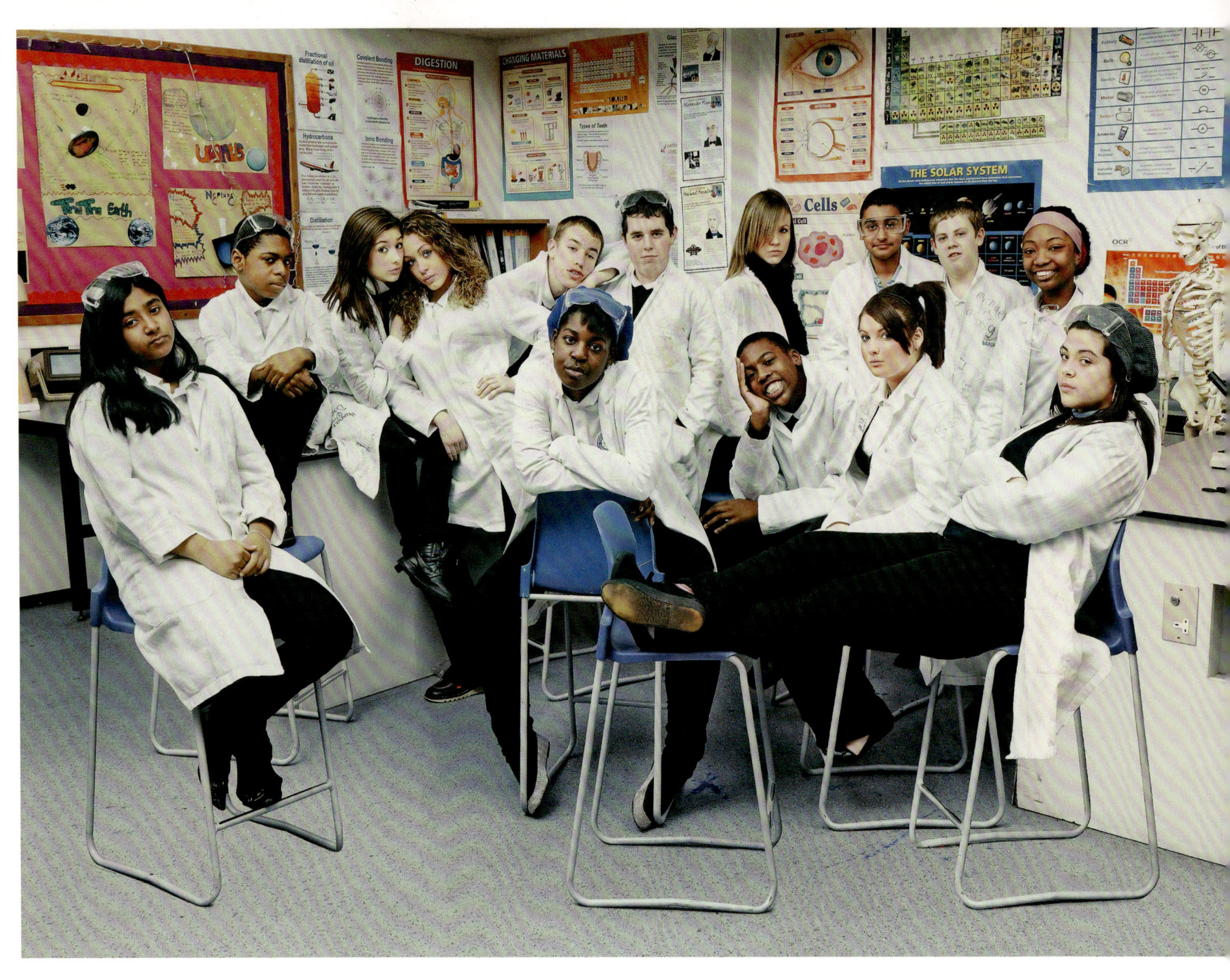

PAUL THOMPSON

SCHOOL KIDS

DECEMBER 2007

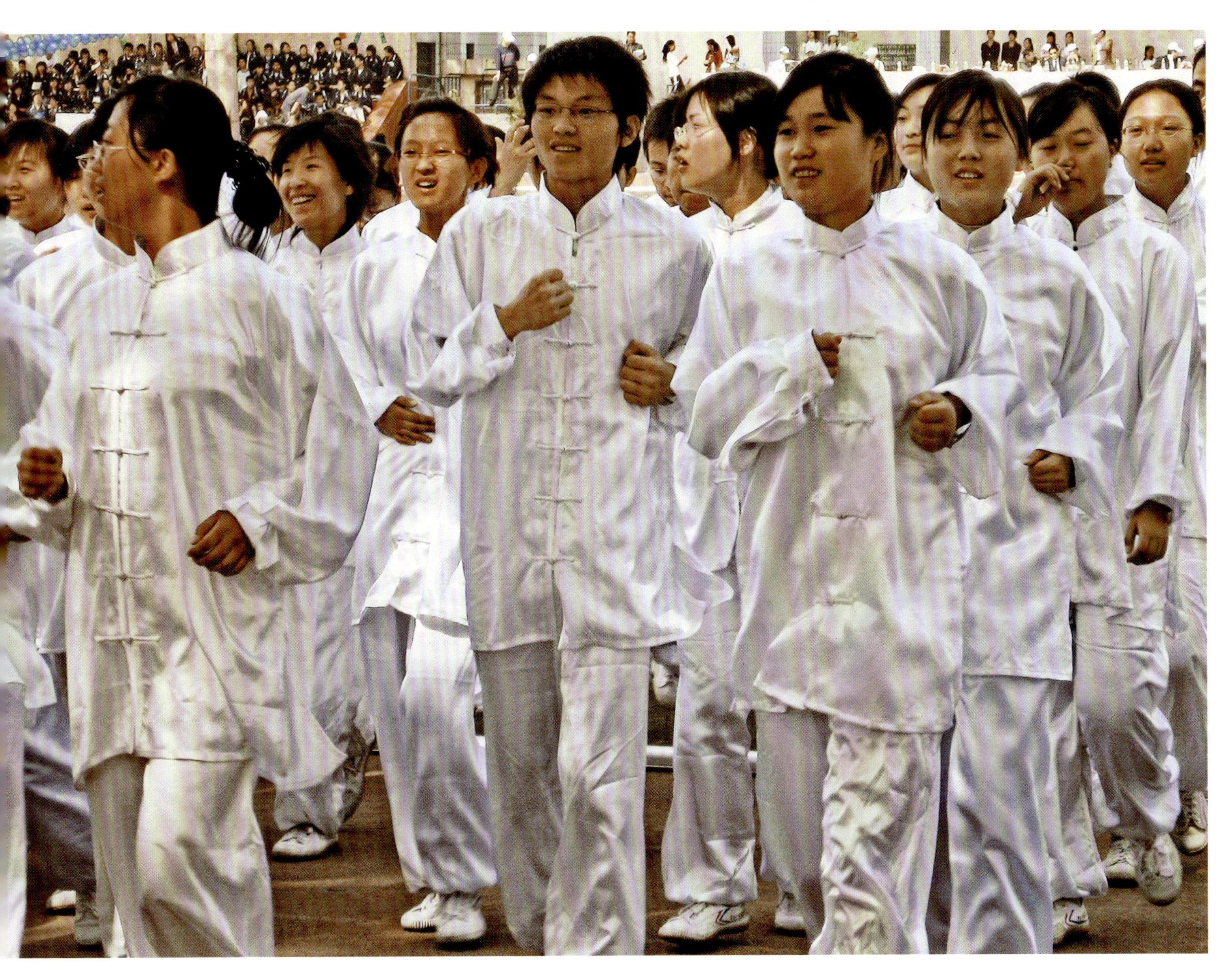

ALASTAIR FAULKNER
TAI CHI CHUAN STUDENTS AT A MEET, XI'AN
APRIL 2007

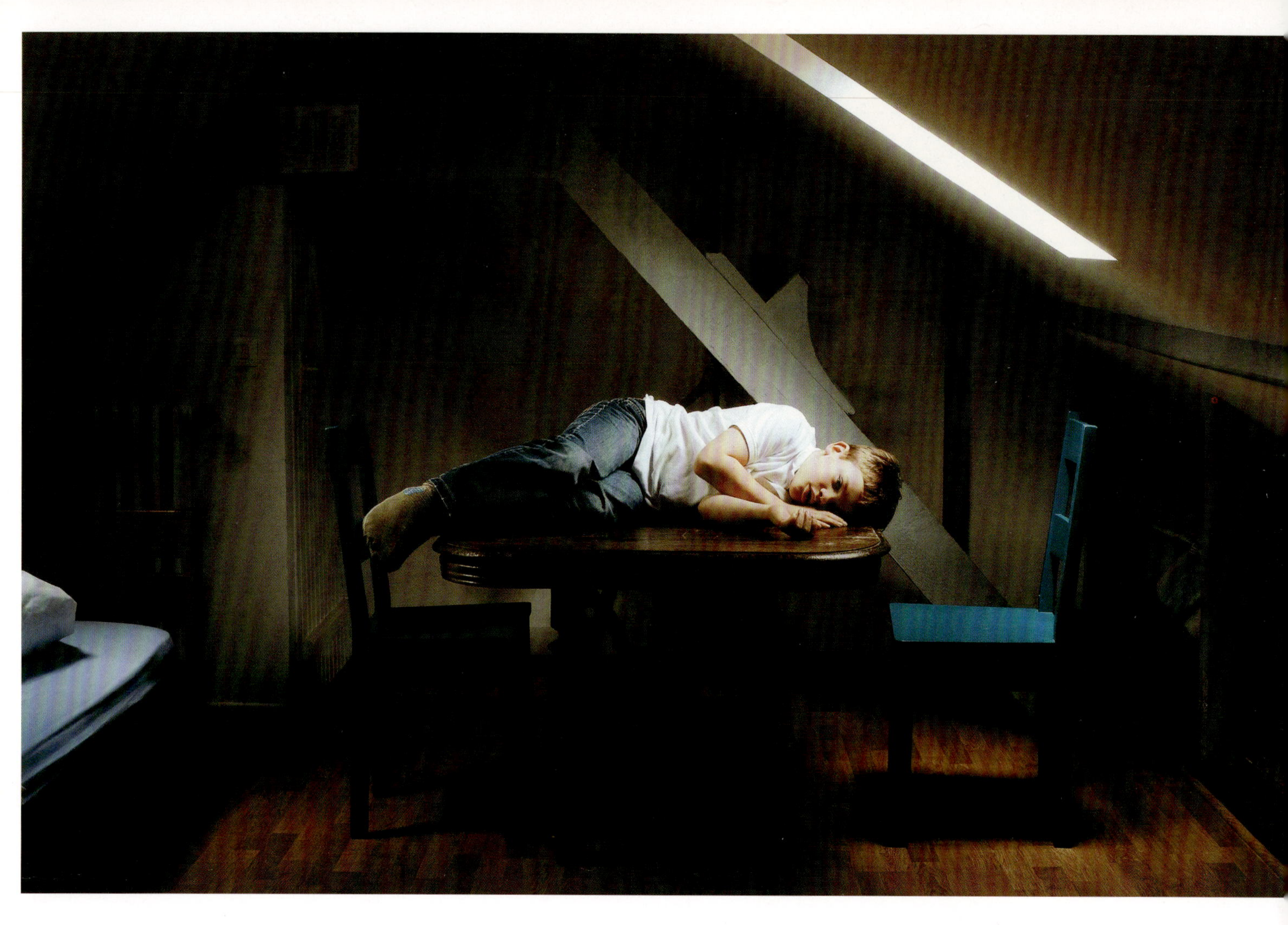

ANNIE COLLINGE
WILLIAM
APRIL 2008

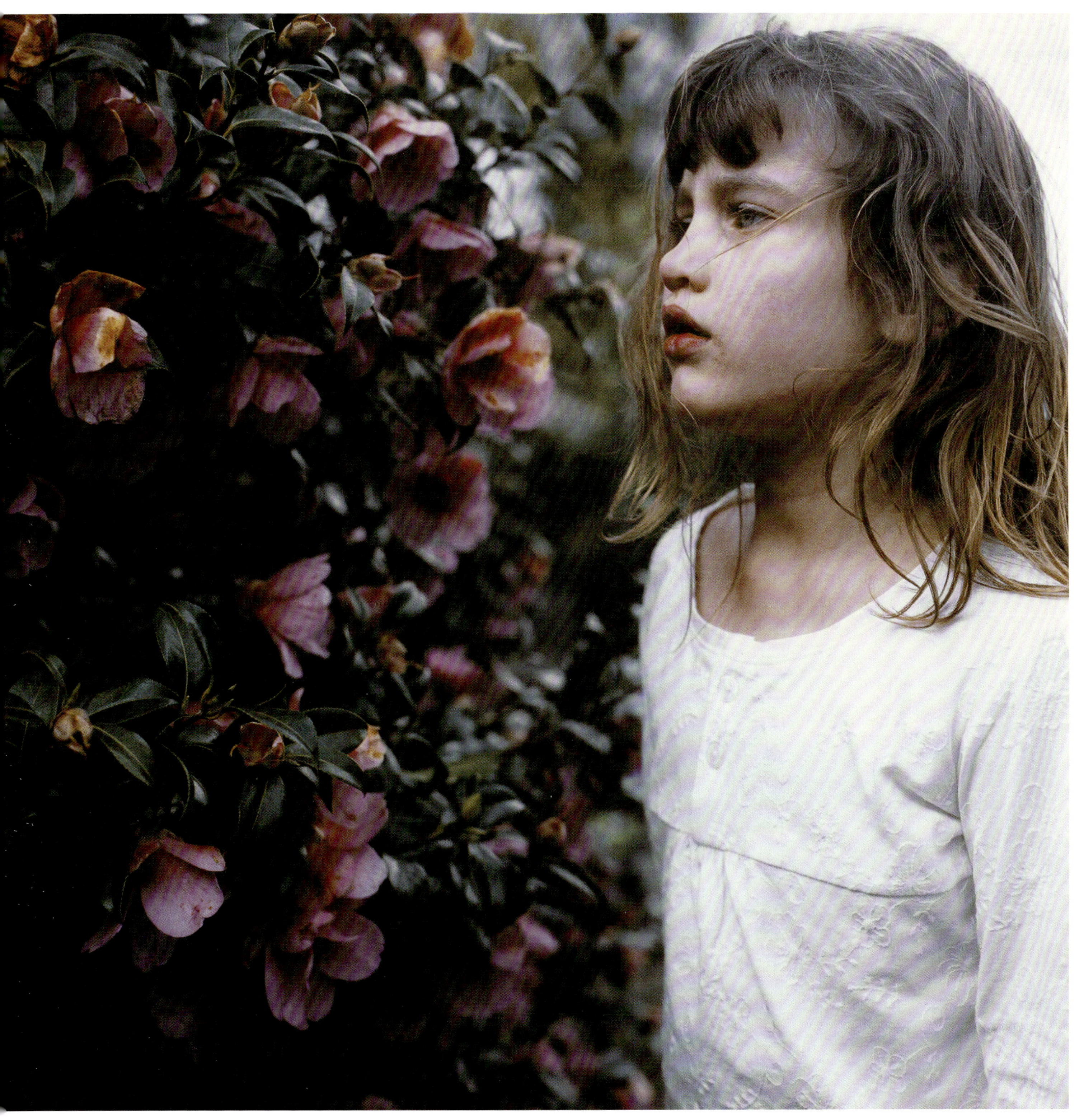

COLIN PANTALL
ISABEL WITH CAMELLIA ON EASTER SUNDAY
FROM THE SERIES *FLORA*
MARCH 2008

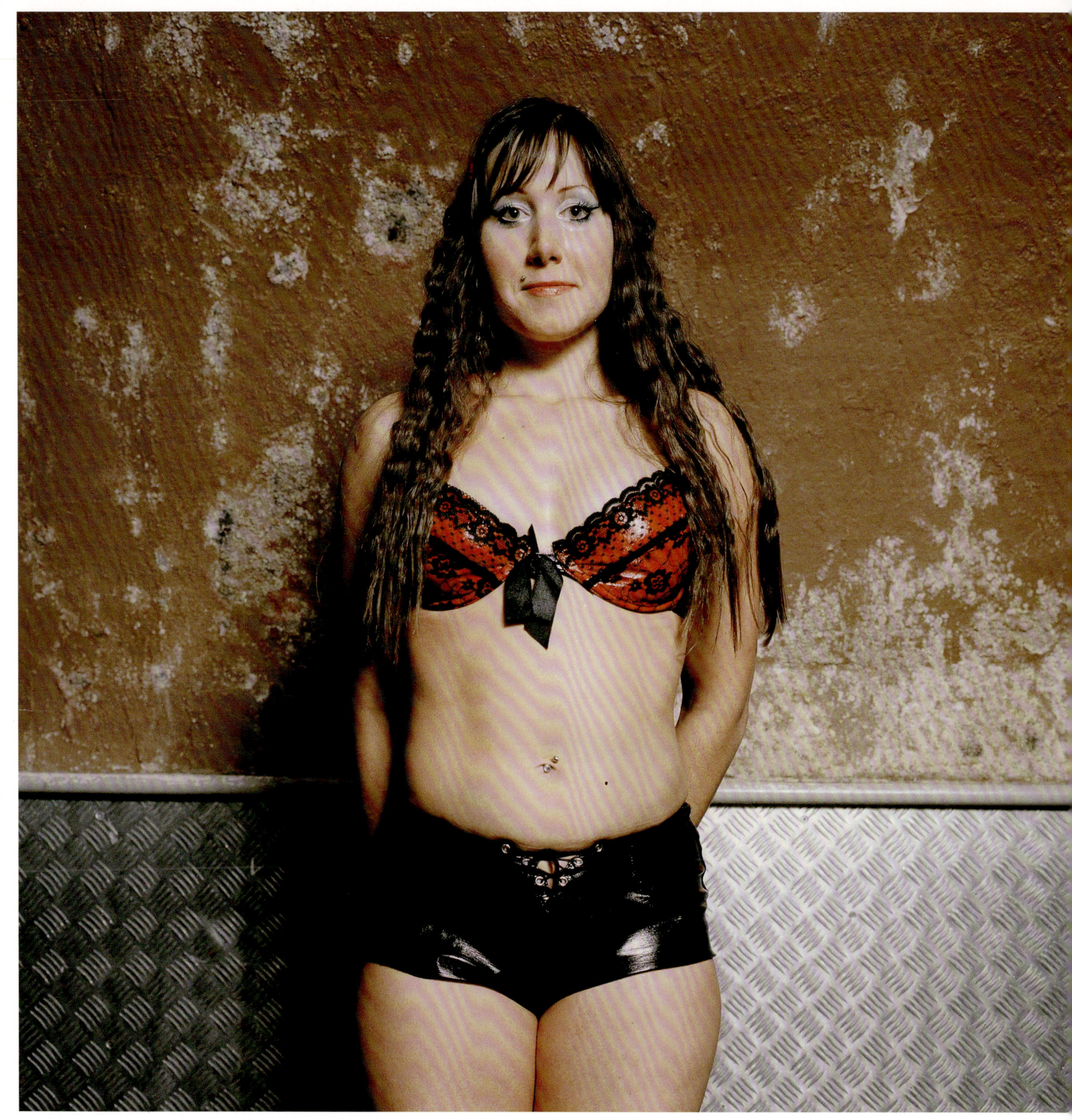

CLAIRE PEPPER

HARMONY
FROM THE SERIES *MISS POLE DANCE*
OCTOBER 2007

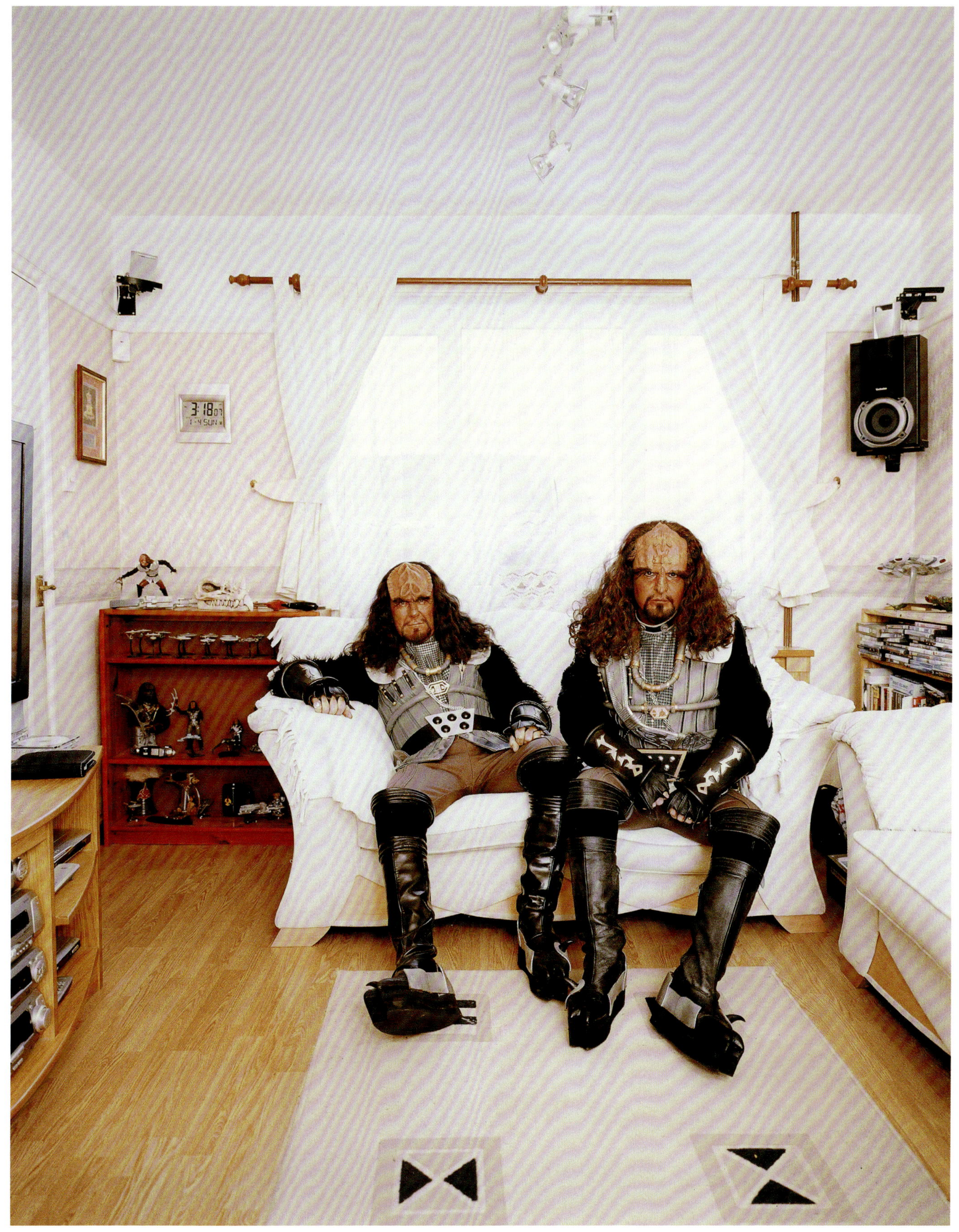

LIST OF EXHIBITORS